"This superb psychoanalytic book evidences the rigour of Freudian metapsychology, its expression in contemporary clinical practice, and the theoretical developments that it inspires. The chapters attest to the implications of taking into account the movement of the drives, of love and hate, life and death: the sexual is always there, in its most archaic or elaborated forms. However, the negative is also present and active in the author's elaborations. A profound knowledge of the Freudian oeuvre and a creative reading of his work are expressed in the depths of a remarkable clinical experience exposed by Perelberg in such a masterful and subtle way. There is no doubt: this is a psychoanalyst who is alive and vibrant—alive in the construction of her concepts and her method, anchored in the original foundations, and yet open to further contributions. The transference, this remarkable Freudian discovery, lends the author its force and meaning as she follows her internal paths of images and words."

Catherine Chabert, Training Analyst, French Psychoanalytical Association; Emeritus Professor, University Paris-Descartes

"This scholarly, impressively intelligent *tour de force* starts with a meticulous exposition of Freud's insights on sexuality, offers clear and vivid syntheses of his clinical cases, and considers further theoretical developments. Perelberg examines in detail contemporary views on the sexual psyche, with contributions from her own recent work and that of other influential psychoanalysts. The book is enriched by her background in anthropology and her interest in culture through connections with literature, art, music, cinema."

Ignês Sodré, Training and Supervising Analyst, British Psychoanalytical Society

Sexuality, Excess, and Representation

Sexuality, Excess, and Representation develops a psychoanalytic understanding of psychic bisexuality and how it can be understood theoretically and in clinical practice.

Rosine Jozef Perelberg articulates a Freudian metapsychology with modern preoccupations with questions of sexual difference and differences. She expands on the ideas presented in her previous edited work, *Psychic Bisexuality: A British–French Dialogue*. The author's approach brings back into focus Freud's idea that "one is not born already made as a man or woman, but one is constituted as such in the process of development". Freud's theoretical writing on bisexuality is examined, returning us firmly to infantile sexuality and the Oedipus complex and the "repudiation of femininity".

Perelberg draws on her past training as a social anthropologist to propose and explore the differentiation between sex, gender, and sexuality. She considers post-war academic work in gender and women's studies and queer theory, arguing that the object of psychoanalysis is not gender but sexuality, which establishes a link between the sexual and the unconscious. She suggests that the unconscious permanently challenges our apparent unity as subjects.

Sexuality, Excess, and Representation will be of great interest to all practising psychoanalysts and psychoanalytic psychotherapists.

Rosine Jozef Perelberg is President of the British Psychoanalytical Society, Visiting Professor in the Psychoanalysis Unit at University College London, and Corresponding Member of the Paris Psychoanalytical Society. Prior to embarking on psychoanalysis she received a PhD in Social Anthropology from the London School of Economics. Her books include *Psychoanalytic Understanding of Violence and Suicide, Female Experience: Four Generations of British Women Psychoanalysts on Work with Women* (with Joan Raphael-Leff), *Time and Memory, Dreaming and Thinking, The Greening of Psychoanalysis* (with Gregorio Kohon), and *Psychic Bisexuality: A British–French Dialogue*. She is the author of *Time, Space and Phantasy* and *Murdered Father, Dead Father: Revisiting the Oedipus Complex*. She works in London in private practice.

THE NEW LIBRARY OF PSYCHOANALYSIS

General Editor: Alessandra Lemma

The New Library of Psychoanalysis was launched in 1987 in association with the Institute of Psychoanalysis, London. It took over from the International Psychoanalytical Library, which published many of the early translations of the works of Freud and the writings of most of the leading British and Continental psychoanalysts.

The purpose of the New Library of Psychoanalysis is to facilitate a greater and more widespread appreciation of psychoanalysis and to provide a forum for increasing mutual understanding between psychoanalysts and those working in other disciplines, such as the social sciences, medicine, philosophy, history, linguistics, literature, and the arts. It aims to represent different trends both in British psychoanalysis and in psychoanalysis generally. The New Library of Psychoanalysis is well placed to make available to the English-speaking world psychoanalytic writings from other European countries and to increase the interchange of ideas between British and American psychoanalysts. Through the *Teaching Series*, the New Library of Psychoanalysis now also publishes books that provide comprehensive, yet accessible, overviews of selected subject areas aimed at those studying psychoanalysis and related fields such as the social sciences, philosophy, literature, and the arts.

The Institute, together with the British Psychoanalytical Society, runs a low-fee psychoanalytic clinic, organizes lectures and scientific events concerned with psychoanalysis, and publishes the *International Journal of Psychoanalysis*. It runs a training course in psychoanalysis which leads to membership of the International Psychoanalytical Association—the body which preserves internationally agreed standards of training, of professional entry, and of professional ethics and practice for psychoanalysis as initiated and developed by Sigmund Freud. Distinguished members of the Institute have included Michael Balint, Wilfred Bion, Ronald Fairbairn, Anna Freud, Ernest Jones, Melanie Klein, John Rickman, and Donald Winnicott.

Previous general editors have included David Tuckett, who played a very active role in the establishment of the New Library.

He was followed as general editor by Elizabeth Bott Spillius, who was in turn followed by Susan Budd and then by Dana Birksted-Breen. Current members of the Advisory Board include Giovanna Di Ceglie, Liz Allison, Anne Patterson, Josh Cohen, and Daniel Pick.

Previous members of the Advisory Board include Christopher Bollas, Ronald Britton, Catalina Bronstein, Donald Campbell, Rosemary Davies, Sara Flanders, Stephen Grosz, John Keene, Eglé Laufer, Alessandra Lemma, Juliet Mitchell, Michael Parsons, Rosine Jozef Perelberg, Richard Rusbridger, Mary Target, and David Taylor.

For a full list of all the titles in the New Library of Psychoanalysis main series as well as both the New Library of Psychoanalysis "Teaching" and "Beyond the Couch" subseries, please visit the Routledge website.

Sexuality, Excess, and Representation

A Psychoanalytic Clinical and Theoretical Perspective

Rosine Jozef Perelberg

Routledge
Taylor & Francis Group
LONDON AND NEW YORK

First published 2020
by Routledge
2 Park Square, Milton Park, Abingdon, Oxon OX14 4RN

and by Routledge
52 Vanderbilt Avenue, New York, NY 10017

Routledge is an imprint of the Taylor & Francis Group, an informa business

British Library Cataloguing-in-Publication Data
A catalogue record for this book is available from the British Library

Library of Congress Cataloging-in-Publication Data
A catalog record has been requested for this book

ISBN: 978-0-367-25354-7 (hbk)
ISBN: 978-0-367-25355-4 (pbk)
ISBN: 978-0-429-28733-6 (ebk)

Typeset in Bembo
by Swales & Willis, Exeter, Devon, UK

To Sergio, my partner in this journey.

Contents

Acknowledgements

The opening chapter of this book, "Psychoanalytic Understanding of Bisexuality: A Framework", first written as an introduction to *Psychic Bisexuality: A British–French Dialogue* (2018), is derived from the seminars on sexuality that I have run for over 20 years at the Psychoanalysis Unit at University College London. I am grateful to all the staff and colleagues at the Psychoanalysis Unit for their continuous support for my seminars.

This chapter is also an expression of a conversation between British and French colleagues. The British–French colloquia have, over the last two decades, been attended by many friends and colleagues, and we now continue this dialogue in different contexts, including the Congrès de Psychanalystes de Langue Française (CPLF). I am grateful to George Pragier and Evelyne Chauvet, who first invited me to present at the CPLF, and now to Marilia Aisenstein and Bernard Chervert, for their annual invitations to these events. This chapter has been expanded to incorporate my introduction, in 2017, to the Colloquium on Sexuality at the Anna Freud National Centre for Children and Families.

"On Excess, Trauma, and Helplessness: Repetitions and Transformations" was first presented as the keynote address to the Deutsche Psychoanalytische Gesellschaft (DPG) Congress, in Dusseldorf, in 2014. Over 22 years, friends and colleagues from the DPG have often been the first forum for dialogue on my emergent ideas. The chapter was then discussed as part of a gripping day dialogue with Jean Claude Rolland, organized by Olivier Bonard at the Lausanne Psychoanalytical Society in 2014, and also read at the Scientific Meeting of the British Psychoanalytical Society in March 2015.

"Negative Hallucinations, Dreams, and Hallucinations: The Framing Structure and Its Representation in the Analytic Setting" was written for the conference held at the Institute of Psychoanalysis in honour of André Green and was originally published in the 2017 collection co-edited with Gregorio Kohon, entitled *The Greening of Psychoanalysis*. This was a celebratory occasion, when we counted with the presence of Litza Guttieres-Green. Part of the chapter was also presented at the Congrès des Psychanalystes de Langue Française in Paris in 2016.

"Love and Melancholia in the Analysis of Women by Women" was presented to the Contemporary Freudian Tradition Conference of Sexuality at the British Psychoanalytical Society, in May 2018. This was a vibrant day of exchanges, with the participation of Marilia Aisenstein, Rachel Chaplin, Jed Sekoff, and Gregorio Kohon.

"The Riddle of Anxiety: Between the Familiar and the Unfamiliar" was one of the key addresses to the University College London Conference on Anxiety, Dread, Fear in December 2017. I am grateful to David Taylor for his invitation to present this paper at the conference. It was then the focus of a two-month online discussion, organized by Gustavo Jarast, with my Spanish-speaking colleagues. I am most grateful to all who participated in this fruitful forum of exchanges.

"The Uncanny and the Beginnings of Time in *One Hundred Years of Solitude*" was first presented in November 2018 at the Conference on The Uncanny: Art, Literature and the Clinic, organized with Ignês Sodré and Gregorio Kohon, at the British Psychoanalytical Society. It is a development of a paper originally written with Bella Jozef and published in 2008 in the book *Time, Space and Phantasy*, also in the New Library of Psychoanalysis.

An intellectual and clinical trajectory takes place in a process of conversation. I am fortunate to have encountered, over the years, inspiring friends and colleagues—too many to name—in Britain and many other parts of the world, and I am very grateful to each of them. I also wish to express my thanks to my students who have attended my seminars at University College London and at the Institute of Psychoanalysis and my private postgraduate seminars, for always asking challenging questions and for their contribution to my thinking.

Donald Campbell and Gregorio Kohon are close interlocutors in our continuous dialogue, which has been taking place over a long period.

My patients are at the heart of everything, and I am continuously humbled by their trust in me.

I thank Eric and Klara King for the careful editing of the manuscripts and for their infinite patience and availability.

I thank the *International Journal of Psychoanalysis* for permission to reprint the following papers:

"On Excess, Trauma and Helplessness: Repetition and Transformations", *International Journal of Psychoanalysis, 96*: 1453–1476.

"Negative Hallucinations, Dreams and Hallucinations: The Framing Structure and Its Representation in the Analytic Setting", *International Journal of Psychoanalysis, 97* (No. 6, 2016): 1575–1590.

"Love and Melancholia in the Analysis of Women by Women", *International Journal of Psychoanalysis, 98* (No. 6, 2017): 1533–1549.

"The Riddle of Anxiety: Between the Familiar and the Unfamiliar", *International Journal of Psychoanalysis, 99* (No. 4, 2018): 810–827.

I thank Routledge for permission to reproduce the "Introduction" to *Psychic Bisexuality: A British–French Dialogue* (London: Routledge, 2016); also, parts of a chapter written with Bella Jozef: R. J. Perelberg & B. Jozef, "Time and Memory in *One Hundred Years of Solitude*", in R. J. Perelberg, *Time, Space and Phantasy* (London: Routledge, 2008), pp. 153–162.

I am grateful to the Centre National de Préhistoire of the French Minister of Culture for permission to reproduce one of the pictures from the Grotte Chauvet-Pont-d'Arc (Ardèche)

Panneau du Mégacéros, Galerie des Mégacéros © V. Feruglio/MC.

INTRODUCTION

A psychoanalytic understanding of sexuality refers to unconscious phantasies and infantile sexuality, defined by transgression and incestuous desires that are repressed and repudiated, defying the possibility of them ever being fully known. There is a radical discontinuity between the unconscious and knowledge. From his "Project" (1950 [1895]), written in 1895 but published after his death, to the *Outline of Psychoanalysis* (1940 [1938]), Freud attempted to explore the relationship between the drives and their representations, the somatic and the psychic, positing a discontinuity between the two. Already in *Studies on Hysteria* (1895d), sexuality is conceived as traumatic, because of its excessive nature. Corporeal experiences are at the very origin of the constitution of the psyche, and it is only progressively and *incompletely* that they become constituted as psychic reality.

In 1920 Freud postulated the existence of a drive that does not correspond to any representation but is expressed though the repetition compulsion (1920g). The structural model of the mind instituted a close relationship between the id and the soma. The id is described as "chaos, a cauldron full of seething excitations" (1933a, p. 73). Psychoanalytic work is concerned with the way the experience of an infantile traumatic past, in its unmetabolizable aspects, may present itself in the consulting room. If the drives are at the root of psychic activity, this "implies that something is basically *in excess*, an overload charge on the mind, linked with the bodily exigencies of the drives whose derivatives have to be sent back to the unconscious because their free expression forbids psychic organisation" (Green, 1998, p. 660).

Freud is part of a philosophical tradition that emphasizes the absence and the negative. A presence in language is already related to absence. As Lacan put it, "The symbol manifests itself first of all as the murder of the thing, and this death constitutes in the subject the eternalization of its desire" (Lacan, 1977, p. 104). If one takes these ideas seriously, the implication is that psychoanalysis can only very imprecisely give meaning to the unconscious, which is only reached through its derivatives. There is something in excess that can never be fully grasped. The implicit danger for any psychoanalytic discourse is that of reducing heterogeneity (Shaviro, 1990, p. 70)—and, I would add, complexity—to representation.

In the consulting room one is confronted with this experience of excess that refers to the drives, to the sexual, that is only incompletely transformed into psychic reality.

At the heart of all the chapters is the relationship of body and drive to psychic representation. The discussion interweaves themes of body, sexuality, and excess, illustrating and demonstrating the centrality of psychosexuality.

Chapter 1 develops a psychoanalytic understanding of psychic bisexuality. It articulates the preoccupation of Freudian metapsychology with questions of sexual difference and differences. It is an expansion of a previous introduction to my book, *Psychic Bisexuality: a British–French Dialogue* (Perelberg, 2018b). The approach is to bring back into focus Freud's idea that one is not born already made as a man or woman, but one is constituted as such in the process of development. Freud's theoretical writing on bisexuality is examined, returning us firmly to infantile sexuality, the Oedipus complex, and the "repudiation of femininity". I draw on my past training as a social anthropologist to explore the differentiation between sex, gender, and sexuality. I also consider post-war academic work in gender and women's studies and queer theory: the object of psychoanalysis is not gender but sexuality, which establishes a link between the sexual and the unconscious, as "the unconscious never ceases to challenge our apparent unity as subjects" (Rose, 1982, p. 30). The subsequent discussion of transsexuals deepens the engagement of an analytic contribution beyond the cul-de-sac of psychotic delusion: in psychoanalysis, taking into account the fluidity of identifications, it is clear that absolute certainty about one's identifications expresses a confusion of registers—addressing as real something that belongs to the symbolic sphere.

Chapter 2, "On Excess, Trauma, and Helplessness: Repetitions and Transformations", explores the links between an excessive amount of excitation, the infant's experience of helplessness, and trauma. The idea of excess emphasizes a quantitative element not reducible to the field of representation. Patients who create full or empty spaces in the analyst's mind are described in clinical detail, a further exploration of a distinction I previously made (Perelberg, 2003). A patient who lived through experiences of excess and flooding is contrasted with another patient whose experience of excess is expressed through withdrawal. The complex process of elaboration and working through takes place in their analyses by bringing together affect, representation, sensorial and somatic experiences, dreams, associations, and enactments as they are gathered and given meaning *après coup* through analytic work. The chapter emphasizes the place of temporality in creating a triadic space in an analysis as it relates the *here and now* with the *there and then* in the work of *après-coup*.

Chapter 3 explores the meaning of a patient's hallucinatory experiences in the course of a five-times-a-week analysis and places it within the pre-oedipal domain, the primary relationship to the mother. An understanding of the transference and countertransference was crucial in the creation of meaning and the enabling of the transformations that took place in the analytic process. Through a detailed analysis of a clinical example, I examine Bion's distinction between *hysterical hallucinations* and *psychotic hallucinations* and formulate my own hypothesis about the distinctions between the two. The chapter suggests that while psychotic hallucinations express a conflict between *life* and *death*, in hysterical hallucination the conflict is between *love* and *hate*. The chapter also offers some reflections on the *dramatic* nature of the analytic encounter.

The negative hallucination of the mother is a precondition for Freud's hallucinatory wish-fulfilment, for images, for phantasy life, and for thinking. It is also an indication of thirdness, as the mother's absence implicitly poses the question: "Where does she go when she goes away?" This is an implicit reference to the father. It is to him, as her lover, that she goes. The mother's absence, and the activity of phantasy that her absence gives rise to within the framing structure, lies at the heart of my ideas about the psychoanalytic setting itself, as discussed in this chapter.

What happens if these processes fail to take place and a traumatic intrusion does not allow for absence, which would enable a psychic space to be solidly constituted? What are the consequences for the beginnings of phantasy life if the mother is too terrifying for the child, as the psychotic mother might be, so that the child cannot internalize its framing structure?

In the treatment of non-neurotic patients, one is dealing not with an economy of unconscious desire, but with a "logic of despair". This logic is less organized than that of the primary process and has to contend with unprocessed elements coming from the id. Thinking is dominated by the work of the negative. The aim of analytic work is to transform hallucinations into words that create a narrative about the patient's history, transforming delirium into play and death into absence.

In Chapter 4, "Love and Melancholia in the Analysis of Women by Women", a very vivid clinical case again brings us to the centre of excess, the body, and passion. The chapter takes up the distinctive aspect of women working with women when it presents an overwhelming reappearance and an expression of the core conflict of passion for the mother and a wish for and dread of fusion. What is also a source of struggle is the primary erotic and ambivalent relationship to the mother. I suggest that a crucial dimension that is present in the analyses of these female patients is a struggle with a melancholic core that cannot be elaborated. To clarify: the core of melancholia is the murder of the primordial object that is lost for ever and yet, in a way, never lost entirely, because the subject will always be attempting to find it again. The emergence of this melancholic core becomes a construction in the *après-coup* of an analysis.

Chapter 5, "The Riddle of Anxiety: Between the Familiar and the Unfamiliar", underlines that at the core of the experience of anxiety is the original experience of helplessness. Anxiety is an affective state that is accompanied by physical sensations and bodily symptoms—expression of an *excess* that it is not possible to process psychically. Anxiety is also linked to the fear of loss of the imaginary integrity of the body, as well as of primary objects. Furthermore, anxiety marks the passage from the world of the narcissistic father and/or mother, in which the individual is alienated from his or her own history, to the dead father configuration, which inserts the individual into a subjective temporality in the *après-coup* of an analysis. A detailed narrative of an analysis that gave rise to these ideas is presented. In this analysis the transsexual emerges to give shape to something that had not previously reached representation.

This chapter presents another view of the theme of the book itself in the complexity of a transference that brings alive the primeval chaos of the unconscious, or the reality of Lacan's mirror-stage emphasis on the illusion of the unified self.

Chapter 6, on "The Uncanny and the Beginning of Time in *One Hundred Years of Solitude*", suggests that Freud's "The 'Uncanny'" (1919h) raises questions about the primal scene, the maternal and the paternal, the sexual of the feminine and the masculine, and the puzzle about the question of what happens at night between the parents. It refers to incestuous desires that are frightening, forbidden, and disgusting. In the analysis of the original Hoffmann story of the Sandman, I revisit my distinction between the nurturing, "day" father and the diabolical "night" father, who is the mother's lover—the embodiment of the father in the primal scene. Is it that the act of sex is, by definition, uncanny because of the experience that "one has, therefore, been there before"? Is incest at the core of the riddle of anxiety?

The analysis is centred on Gabriel García Márquez's novel, *One Hundred Years of Solitude*, now revisited through the lens of the uncanny. The novel deals with major universal mysteries: search for one's origins, incest, endogamy, separation, procreation, death. More specifically, it depicts a relationship between time and the formation of a couple that takes 100 years, which has allowed the author to write a novel that has become a myth of origins.

I suggest that this is also the stuff of an analysis that consistently presents us with uncanny experiences that take us back to the beginnings of time in the here and now and the expression of a phantasy—very frequently strange and terrifying—that has never existed before.

Part I

A THEORETICAL FRAMEWORK TOWARDS THE UNDERSTANDING OF PSYCHOSEXUALITY

1

PSYCHOANALYTIC UNDERSTANDING OF BISEXUALITY

A framework

> Although, for psychoanalysis, difference is sexual, the question of bisexuality is related to psychoanalytic theory as a whole.
>
> (A. Green, 2001, p. 158)

> A King of shreds and patches.
>
> (Shakespeare, *Hamlet*, III: iv, l. 103)

Initial considerations

I wish to offer a few lines of thought at the outset:

- The second half of the twentieth and the early twenty-first centuries have been marked by the emergence of the cyborg—a hybrid creature, made up of both organism and machine. This is the inauguration of a world in which, because of the penetration of technology into the very construction of the human body, the traditional philosophical and anthropological dichotomies between nature and culture, humans and objects, men and women no longer appear to offer a framework for understanding the world. If these considerations indicate a need to take into account the technological, social, and political forms that inform the practices existing within contemporary societies, how do these categorizations impact our psychoanalytic thinking on sexuality?—Or do they?

- A psychoanalytic understanding of sexuality refers to the *unconscious, repressed* aspects of sexuality, which have their origins in *infantile sexuality* and can only be derived *après-coup* in the analytic process.
- Psychoanalysis has, since Freud, viewed sexuality in itself as *traumatic* to the individual. This traumatic dimension is linked to the force of the drives in that there is always something *in excess* that cannot be reduced to the level of representation (Perelberg, 2015). This excessive aspect of sexuality has been highlighted in different ways by Bataille (1957), Kohon (1999), and Laplanche (1987).
- The traumatic dimension of sexuality also relates to the recognition of the difference between the sexes, the result of a long process of development and elaboration. In its homosexual and heterosexual dimensions, the oedipal configuration confronts the child with the impossibility of belonging to both sexes, as well as the impossibility of possessing their parents. This establishes a link between sexuality, castration, renunciation, taboo, and prohibition (Perelberg, 2009b).
- The revolutionary contribution made by Freud is the idea that one is not born already formed as a man or woman, but one is *constituted* as such in the process of development.
- There is a fundamental difference between a psychoanalytic perspective on sexuality and a sociological definition of gender.
- In the psychoanalytic movement, there has been a process of *de-sexualization* of the theory (Green, 1986c; Kohon, 1999).

Psychic bisexuality

In a letter to Fliess in 1896, Freud used the word "bisexuality" for the first time:

> In order to account for why the outcome [of premature sexual experience] … is sometimes perversion and sometimes neurosis, I avail myself of the bisexuality of all human beings.
>
> (Freud, 1950 [1892–1899], p. 238)

Freud was to use the term "bisexuality" 44 times throughout his work. In the initial phase, he was still concerned with matching his ideas on bisexuality to the anatomical–biological substratum proposed by Fliess, to whom he attributed the discovery of bisexuality. It is only progressively that bisexuality acquired a more fundamental psychological meaning in his work. In time Freud came to regard bisexuality as an inherent characteristic of all human beings.

In his *Studies on Hysteria* (1895d), Freud established an essential link between hysteria and bisexuality. He suggested that hysterical attacks express an experience of rape in which the hysteric plays both roles.[1] "In one case I observed, for instance, the patient pressed her dress up against her body with one hand (as a woman), while she tried to tear it off with the other (as a man)" (Freud, 1908a, p. 166).

It was in his discussion of the case of Katharina in 1896 that Freud himself first related hysteria to the primal scene (Letter 52, in Freud, 1950 [1892–1899]). Freud mentioned at least three further cases linking anxiety to the primal scene—in a letter to Fliess, in his paper on anxiety neurosis (1895b), and in his analysis of Dora (1905e). Later, in a letter to Jung on 21 November 1909, Freud wrote about Anna O's term "chimney sweeping":

> The reason why a chimney sweep is supposed to bring good luck is that sweeping a chimney is an unconscious symbol of coitus, which is something of which Breuer certainly never dreamed.
>
> (in McGuire, 1974, p. 267)

The hysteric is the feminine in the neurotic representation (Schaeffer, 1986); it is also the very repudiation of the feminine. Kohon has suggested a divalent stage for the hysteric: "In fact, stuck in her divalent stage, the hysteric … cannot define herself as a man or as a woman because she cannot finally choose between her father and her mother" (Kohon, 1999, p. 19).

Schaeffer—using an expression coined by Michel Cachoux (see Schaeffer, 1997)—suggests that the hysteric, like a ruby, displays what it is in fact rejecting: "The ruby is a stone that has a horror of red. It absorbs and retains all the other colours, but rejects and expels red" (Schaeffer, 1986, p. 925). Thus, the hysteric has a horror of the colour red, of sexuality, while at the same time displaying it. In her hysterical pregnancy Anna O was, paradoxically, rejecting a feminine identification—the woman who would produce babies as a result of intercourse.

Some aspects of Bertha Pappenheim's later life represent transformations of Anna O's question, "Am I a man or a woman?" (see Kohon, 1984; Lacan, 1993; Leclaire, 1980), albeit in a sublimated way. In her social work, she designated the social workers she trained as her daughters—products of an imaginary intercourse without a father or mother. The orphanage she built was known as "Papahome"—the house of the father—in which she would fulfil the two parental roles.

Hysteria becomes, fundamentally, a mode of thinking about sexuality and the sexual object (Schaeffer, 1986).[2] Hysteria works by imitation; the difference between identification and imitation is that between "being like the object" and "being the object". Through her symptoms, Anna O seems to be *imitating* the sexual act. *Her symptoms become like a theatre of the sexual act in an attempt to both deny and represent the primal scene and deny the mourning of her incestuous sexual desires.* It is also displaying a body that cannot be experienced as sexual and feminine, but only as bits and pieces that ache. The fracture of the mind (the Humpty Dumpty song she recited at her father's bedside) is mirrored in the fragmentation of the body through her symptoms.

Freud's revolutionary vision on sexuality was to maintain the inherent, unconscious, infantile, perverse psychic bisexuality in both men and women. Each child is confronted with questions about the enigma of the differences between the sexes of the parents and the nature of their sexuality (Freud, 1905d, pp. 194–197).

Masculine and feminine are structural positions in relation to the difference between the sexes. The interplay of identifications in relation to the primal scene is implicit or explicit in each of Freud's case studies, from Dora (1905e), to Little Hans (1909b), the Rat Man (1909d), Schreber (1911c), the Wolf Man (1918b), to "The Psychogenesis of a Case of Homosexuality in a Woman" (1920a). I give summarized indications below for some of Freud's clinical cases.

Dora (Freud, 1905e)

The theme of hysteria and its relationship with sexuality continues in the discussion of Dora's analysis, which expresses Freud's interest in the sexual origins of hysterical symptoms, as well as in the role of dreams as expressing unconscious conflicts. The hysterical symptom "enacts a fantasy with a sexual content" (Cournut-Janin, 2005), even if a single unconscious phantasy is generally not sufficient to engender a symptom.

In this analysis Freud is still interested in the reconstruction of the trauma that had led to the appearance of the symptom, through the analysis of dreams and free associations. This clinical emphasis would change in later years, when Freud started to see the analytic process more in terms of a process of construction. At the time of the analysis itself, Freud emphasized the paternal transference and the role of the father's impotence in the structuring of the symptom. Dora's aphonia and cough are understood as manifestations of the unconscious phantasy of having oral sex with a woman, Mrs K, in identification with her impotent father. In Freud's formulations, a symptom establishes a link between unconscious phantasy and sexuality: "a symptom signifies the representation—the realization of a phantasy with a sexual content, that is to say, it signifies a sexual situation" (1905e, p. 47).

There is a link between the current phantasy and a childhood memory, as Dora tells Freud that as a child she had been a thumb-sucker. She remembers an occasion when she would be thumb-sucking at the same time as she would be tugging at her brother's earlobe (p. 51). Freud believes that these are new versions of a "pre-historic impression of sucking at the mother's or nurse's breast" (p. 52).

It is only retrospectively, after Dora had broken off the analysis, that Freud identified the relevance of the maternal transference.

In one of several footnotes added to the text of the analysis of Dora, Freud indicated his mistake in underestimating Dora's love for Frau K: "I failed to discover in time and to inform the patient that her homosexual (gynaecophilic) love for Frau K. was the strongest unconscious current in her mental life" (Freud, 1905e, p. 120).

Yet quite a few years were to pass before Freud discovered the pre-oedipal passion for the mother expressed by children of both sexes. The homosexual love for Frau K would then be seen as the "strongest unconscious current" in the mental life of all individuals. It is always the mother, in the words of Kristeva (2012). Bisexuality was at the core of Freud's understanding of hysteria.

Cournut-Janin (2005) has suggested that

> in the longing for Frau K it is her own femininity that Dora—still an adolescent—also loves the woman she herself will be in the person of the lovely Frau K., who is desirable, as her father has clearly indicated to her.
>
> (2005, p. 58)

From this perspective, Frau K becomes the ideal of unattainable femininity.

More recently, Mitchell has suggested that the identification with the mother is also present in this analysis. Freud himself says that Dora

> identified with her mother by means of slight symptoms and peculiarities of manner, which gave her an opportunity for some really remarkable achievements in the direction of intolerable behaviour. … The persistence with which she held to this identification with her mother almost forced me to ask whether she too was suffering from a venereal disease.
>
> (Mitchell, 2000, pp. 75–76)

At the time, it was believed that syphilis could lead to madness. In her analysis of the case, Mitchell suggests that Freud is both the father and the mother in the transference. She also convincingly emphasizes the importance of Dora's identification with her older brother, Otto Bauer, in the development of Dora's symptoms. "She had wanted to be positioned as a child in the family like her brother, only to discover that she was not like him in gender and that (probably) he, first-born and male, had their mother's love" (Mitchell, 2000, p. 104). Her hysteria emanated from childhood and a "breakdown of her identification *with her brother*" (p. 105).

Little Hans (Freud, 1909b)

This was an analysis carried out by Little Hans's father, Max Graf, who sent Freud extensive notes about his son. When he was 4 years old, Herbert witnessed a cart horse that was pulling a heavy load collapse. The little boy became fearful of horses: Freud understood Hans's phobia as being related to the anxiety caused by the arrival of his younger sister and the lies that the adults were offering him about the origin of babies.

Hans's material offered Freud evidence about his theories on infantile sexuality, castration anxiety, and the Oedipus complex. Progressively, Freud understood Hans's fear as being one of his father biting him (castrating him) for his desires towards the mother. As Hans's father was acting as analyst, Freud conjectured that this fear was impeding the progress of the treatment, so he invited Hans to see him so that he could explain his symptoms to him.

Hans also showed jealousy towards his father and expressed a desire to give his mother babies, thus revealing himself as a "little Oedipus" (Freud, 1909b, p. 11). At the same time, however, his homosexual attachment to his father was recognized. His father described the boy's loving feelings towards boy companions, as well his loving responses to girls. Freud referred to these "accesses of homosexuality" in Hans as one of the many polymorphous libidinal strands that flourished before the effects of repression became evident.

> Hans was a homosexual (as all children may well be), quite consistently with the fact, which must always be kept in mind, that *he was acquainted with one kind of genital organ*—a genital organ like his own.
>
> (Freud, 1909b, p. 110)

Little Hans is an example of the infantile theory of phallic monism that is impermeable to observation. He believed that girls and boys had "widdlers", in spite of the evidence against this through his observation of his sister. This is again an expression of the force of phantasy life and the anxiety provoked by the threat of castration (see a fuller discussion of this later in this chapter).

The account of the case gives ample evidence of Hans's identification with his mother and the wish to give birth to babies, although this is not explored by Freud in the paper and would only be discussed in 1926. As Temperley (2005) indicates, it is only in *Inhibitions, Symptoms and Anxiety* (Freud, 1926d) that Freud linked Hans with the Wolf Man, stating that in both cases the animal phobia derived from tender, passive homosexual desires towards the father, which had been distorted by regression to the oral phase, as well as by repression:

> The process of repression had attacked almost all the components of his Oedipus complex—both his hostile and his tender impulses toward his father and his tender impulses toward his mother.
>
> (Freud, 1926d, p. 107)

In the next paragraph, however, Freud writes:

> A tender feeling for his father was undoubtedly there too and played a part in repressing the opposite feeling: but we can prove neither that it was strong enough to draw repression on itself nor that it disappeared afterwards. Hans seems in fact to have been a normal boy with what is called a "positive" Oedipus complex.
>
> (1926d, p. 107)

The interplay of different desires coexisting within each individual was identified by Freud throughout his work: "The emotional life of man is in general made up of pairs of contraries such as this" (Freud, 1909b, p. 113).

The Rat Man (1909d)

In the Rat Man Freud describes a bright young man whose emotional, sexual, and social development had been severely stunted by obsessional thinking, the roots of which seemed to stretch back into his infancy. He also describes a precocious sexual life: at the age of 4 the Rat Man had undertaken exploration of his governess's genitals.

Freud gives a vivid description of the patient's conflict of identifications, which was reached only "through the painful road of the transference" (Freud, 1909d, p. 209). While Freud had a polite man, with a polite demeanour, on the couch, in his dreams the patient shouted the "grossest and filthiest abuse upon me and my family", expressing his utter fury towards Freud as his father. At times the disjunction between the conscious behaviour and unconscious expressions led the patient to despair as he paced the consulting room. He could not lie in a comfortable position, he would say, while feeling so uncomfortable with what was going on. Further analysis indicated that he was also afraid that Freud would give him a beating, although in light of the later text, "A Child Is Being Beaten" (1919e), one could also understand his longing for it.

There is indeed an account of Lorenz's masturbatory fantasies, where Freud indicates Lorenz's longing for his father and his battles with him—especially over his choice of a girl—and a complex story of a beating by the father in which Lorenz had flown into a fury and following which, he told Freud, he had "become a coward", fearing physical violence. The father had made a comment about his son—that "The child will be either a great man or a great criminal" (1909d, p. 205).

Freud emphasizes Lorenz's disavowed hostile feelings towards his father as having greatly intensified his obsessional illness. It was not only a conflict between love and hate that drove Lorenz's illness: it was made particularly complex by pleasure, shame, and disgust at the feelings and ideas associated with the conflict.

> There can be no question that there was something in the sphere of sexuality that stood between the father and son, and that the father had come into some sort of opposition to the son's prematurely developed erotic life. Several years after his father's death, the first time he experienced the pleasurable sensations of copulation, an idea sprang into his mind: "This is glorious! One might murder one's father for this!" This was at once an echo and an elucidation of the obsessional ideas of his childhood. Moreover, his father, shortly before his death, had directly opposed what later became our patient's dominating passion. He had noticed that his son was always in the lady's company, and had advised him to keep away from her, saying that it was imprudent of him and that he would only make a fool of himself.
>
> (1909d, p. 201)

Lorenz's episodes of masturbation took place when thinking about his father. Freud understood these as acts of defiance towards this father, who had interfered with the patient's sexual enjoyment, although one cannot avoid considering the homosexual excitement that is also present.

Freud's linking of obsessional thinking to anal eroticism in his understanding of the case is a clinical insight that should not be underestimated, especially given that knowledge of the connection between obsessive–compulsive neurosis and anal regression emerges only in 1926—two decades after Lorenz's analysis (Williams, 2005). As Catherine Chabert suggests, the Rat Man can be regarded as "the very example of the tortures inflicted by object choice and the vicissitudes of psychic bisexuality" (Chabert, 2018).

Ignès Sodré has contributed to the understanding of obsessionality, suggesting that it may be understood as a defence against triangularity. Splitting mechanisms are used in the service of preserving an exclusive two-person relationship with the object. Sodré (1994) suggests a differentiation between two modes of obsessional thinking: in the first the oedipal situation is avoided, and thoughts connected to it are forbidden; the second indicates a configuration on the threshold of the depressive position, whereby the oedipal situation is omnipresent, and thoughts constantly engage in rivalrous battles with each other (1994, p. 380).

In connection with bisexuality, the Rat Man had become frozen at the threshold of the oedipal configuration, unable to elaborate his feelings—either positive or negative—towards his father. Like Freud's other clinical accounts, all written before his discovery of the pre-oedipal phase, one has very little information about the patient's mother, although one can understand his inability to decide between the two ladies in terms of his hesitation about making a sexual choice away from his mother.

The Schreber case (1911c)

In the discussion of the Schreber case, the theme of repressed homosexual desire by a man towards his father appears again. Freud hypothesizes that persecutory anxiety and paranoid delusions are the result of a defence against repressed homosexual desire. Paranoia is the transformation of love into hate, which is then projected onto an external persecutor. The person whom I now hate was at one time loved (Freud, 1911c, p. 41). "I love him" is transformed into "I hate him", which, through the mechanism of projection, becomes "he hates me". "The person he longed for now became his persecutor, and the content of his wishful phantasy became the content of his persecution" (p. 47). At the centre of the paranoid persecution lies an emasculation phantasy, coupled with the idea that he would be transformed into a woman in the act of copulation (see also the discussion of this case by Steiner, 2005).

> The exciting cause of his illness, then was an outburst of homosexual libido; the object of this libido was probably from the very first his doctor, Flechsig; and his struggles against the libidinal impulse produced the conflict which gave rise to the symptom.
>
> (Freud, 1911c, p. 43)

In the following phase, Schreber thought he would be impregnated by divine rays in order to produce a new race of human beings (pp. 20–21). Schreber also refers to a state of bliss, "uninterrupted enjoyment", an "uninterrupted feeling of voluptuousness" (p. 29), achieved through the contemplation of God. In his analysis, Freud establishes a connection between Dr Flechsig, Schreber's physician, God, and his father, and he concludes that the sun is itself a sublimated symbol for the father. "The father's most dreaded threat, castration, actually provided the material for his wishful phantasy … of being transformed into a woman" (p. 56). Yet, at the same time, Freud himself indicates in a footnote that in German the sun is feminine (p. 54), offering the comment that in most languages the sun is masculine. The feminine of the German sun would nevertheless also offer the interpretation of a bisexual, phallic element, before any division between masculine and feminine.

Freud related Schreber's psychosis to what he suggests is the "father complex". One should bear in mind that at this time the concept of the Oedipus complex had not yet been suggested:

> Thus in the case of Schreber we find ourselves once again on the familiar ground of the father-complex. The patient's struggle with Flechsig became revealed to him as a conflict with God, and we must therefore construe it as an infantile conflict with the father whom he loved. … His father's most dreaded threat, castration, actually provided the material for his wishful phantasy (at first resisted but later accepted) of being transformed into a woman.
>
> (Freud, 1911c, pp. 55–56)

Towards the end of his work, Freud developed the concept of the splitting of the ego, which allowed him to develop his views on psychosis from those he had established in the case of Schreber.

The psychotic individual disavows reality and puts aside the role of the symbolic, dead father. Lacan has understood psychosis as the foreclosure of the Name of the Father.

In this text Freud underlines his views on bisexuality once again: "Generally speaking, every human being oscillates all through his life between heterosexual and homosexual feelings, and any frustration or disappointment in the one direction is apt to drive him over into the other" (Freud, 1911c, p. 46).

The Wolf Man (1918b)

In a letter written to Ferenczi in 1913 (quoted in Jones, 1974), Freud reported that the Wolf Man initiated his first session with him by offering to have rectal intercourse with Freud and then to defecate on his head:

> A rich young Russian, whom I took on because of compulsive tendencies, admitted the following transferences to me after the first session: Jewish swindler, he would like to use me from behind and shit on my head. At the age of six years he experienced as his first symptom cursing against God: pig, dog, etc. When he saw three piles of faeces on the street he became uncomfortable because of the Holy Trinity and anxiously sought a fourth in order to destroy the association.
>
> (in Jones, 1974, vol. II, p. 308)

This scene dramatizes a homosexual relationship characterized by anality and the threat of castration: it expresses the patient's state of mind at the beginning of his treatment (see also Perelberg, 2005). There is a repetition at the beginning of the analysis of a trauma that is analogous to that which had activated the anxiety linked to the obsessive symptoms. In his analysis of the statement in that first session, Bokanowski (2010) suggests that the experience of a feminine that is not well internalized in the Wolf Man. He also suggests that phantasies of seduction, castration, and the primal scene are present.

Freud indicated the anal-sadistic regression and cruelty that followed the prohibition of masturbation by the Wolf Man's Nanya (1918b, p. 25): he tormented insects and people, had beating fantasies, and enjoyed mistreating horses. In his disappointment with his

Nanya, he turned to his father as a sexual object (p. 27). Freud had identified serious sadomasochistic trends in the Wolf Man, in his identification with the suffering Christ, and in his beating phantasies and depressive and masochistic self-reproach. This obsessionality appears to have continued until the age of 10. Freud understood the Wolf Man's terror, at the age of 4, of being eaten by the wolves in the famous dream as referring to his conflicting wishes in relation to the father: fear of him on the one hand and unconscious longing for homosexual gratification on the other.

Freud also referred to the Wolf Man in the paper "A Child Is Being Beaten" (1919e). In his sadistic attitudes the Wolf Man identified with his father, but in his masochism "he chose him as a sexual object" (1918b, p. 63). In this period of rumination, the Wolf Man wondered whether Christ had a behind, and Freud understands this as his question as to whether he, himself, could be used by his father as a woman (which reminds us of the very first offer at his first consultation with Freud).

There are three further dreams in this analysis that seem to contain the same conflicts in relation to the Wolf Man's wish to submit erotically to his father. I find it very interesting that the dreams are narrated in a reverse order in the account of the case history: the later dream first, and then, in reverse order, the two others.

When he was about 7 or 8 years old, the Wolf Man was told that on the following day a private teacher would come to give him a lesson.

> That night he dreamt of *his tutor in the shape of a lion that came towards his bed, roaring loudly and in the posture of a wolf, like one he had seen in a children's picture book*: he woke up in a state of anxiety.
>
> (1918b, p. 39, italics added)

Analysis of the dream led to an understanding of his longing to take a passive sexual position in relation to his father.

In a second dream, "*he saw himself riding a horse and pursued by a gigantic caterpillar. He recognized in this dream an allusion to an earlier one from the period before the tutor*" (p. 69, italics added).

In this earlier dream "*he saw the Devil dressed in black and in the upright posture with which the wolf and the lion had terrified him so much in their day. He was pointing with his outstretched finger at a gigantic snail*" (p. 69, italics added).

He associated the Devil to the demon in a well-known poem; the dream itself was a version of a very popular picture representing the demon in a love scene with a girl. The snail was in the woman's place.

The patient remembered a particular event that had occurred a short time before the dream. He had passed by a peasant who was lying, asleep, with his little boy beside him. The latter woke his father. There was also a second recollection, that on the same estate there were trees that were quite white, spun all over by caterpillars. Freud suggests that the patient "took flight from the realization of the phantasy of the son lying with his father, and that he brought in the white trees in order to make an allusion to the anxiety-dream of the white wolves on the walnut tree" (p. 70). Freud understood the dream as expressing the "dread of the feminine attitude towards men against which he had, at first, protected himself via his religious sublimation and was soon to protect himself still more effectively by the military one" (p. 70).

In his remarks to the text, Strachey underlines the "primary feminine impulses" of the Wolf Man:

> The very marked degree of his bisexuality was only a confirmation of views which had long been held by Freud and which dated back to the time of his friendship with Fliess. But in his subsequent writings Freud laid greater stress than before on the fact of the *universal* occurrence of bisexuality and on the existence of an "inverted" or "negative" Oedipus complex. This thesis was given its clearest expression in the passage on the "complete" Oedipus complex in Chapter III of *The Ego and the Id* (1923b). On the other hand, a tempting theoretical inference to the effect that motives related to bisexuality are the invariable determinants of repression is strongly resisted (p. 110 f)—a point to which Freud returned at greater length soon afterwards in "A Child is Being Beaten".
>
> (in Freud, 1918b, p. 6)

In the case of Wolf Man, Freud understands the phobia as ultimately being linked to the fear of castration.

> But it was from fear of being castrated, too, that the little Russian relinquished his wish to be loved by his father, for he thought that a relation of that sort presupposed a sacrifice of his genitals—of the organ which distinguished him from a female. As we see, both forms of the Oedipus complex, the normal, active form and the inverted one, came to grief through the castration complex.
>
> (Freud, 1926d, p. 108)

I have suggested throughout this introduction that the contrasts between passivity/activity, femininity/masculinity, and sadism/masochism are indeed central to Freud's understanding of the structuring of psychic reality in each individual, male or female. They are the axes around which Freud thought about most of his patients, whether hysterics, obsessional neurotics, perverse, or psychotic.

"The psychogenesis of a case of homosexuality in a woman" (1920a)

Freud's 1920 paper, the last of his published clinical studies, is a brief analysis of how an 18-year-old woman came to be homosexual. We are told that she "had aroused displeasure and concern in her parents by the devoted adoration with which she pursued a certain 'society lady' who was about ten years older than herself" (Freud, 1920a, p. 147). The parents claimed that this woman had a notorious reputation and was known to be flagrantly carrying on affairs with both women and men (see also Budd, 2005).

When she was 16, the young girl had developed a maternal inclination and was bitterly disappointed when it was her own mother who gave birth to another brother. Freud believed that the birth of the new baby brother fatally disrupted her own attempts to identify with her mother. Prior to being brought to Freud by her mother, she had attempted suicide by throwing herself over a guard wall beside the railway line (*niederkommen*). Lacan has shown the ambiguity of the word, which, in German, means "coming down" but also "to give birth". The young woman had dreams of becoming a mother, at the same time as her mother had herself given birth to a child by the father.

Several authors have suggested that the interest that the young homosexual girl had in the lady perhaps expressed her identification much more than any sexual desire (e.g., Harris, 1991; Magid, 1993)

In this paper Freud concludes that there is no simple distinction between homosexuals and heterosexuals: "a masculine man, masculine in his erotic life, may nonetheless love only men"; a feminine man, who loves like a woman, may be wholly heterosexual. Similarly for women: physical sexual characteristics, masculinity or femininity, and type of object choice vary independently. All human beings, in addition to their manifest heterosexuality, contain "a very considerable measure of latent or unconscious homosexuality". Human sexual differentiation is multi-factorial; there is not a separate homosexual "third sex".

In many ways, this paper can be seen as the precursor to the papers that were to follow on female sexuality as Freud tackles the passionate, consuming, idealized love that the little girl has towards the lady as a transferential object standing for her mother. Lacan (1994, p. 102) thought the paper was one of the most brilliant of Freud's texts. He pointed out that the young girl desired nothing from the woman, a relationship of no satisfaction that established the relation of lack to this feminine object. She desired in the woman she loved precisely what she did not have herself (p. 110): what she did not have was the phallus.

Freud makes a crucial distinction between sexuality and object choice:

> The literature of homosexuality usually fails to distinguish clearly enough between the questions of the choice of object on the one hand, and of the sexual characteristics and sexual attitude of the subject on the other, as though the answer to the former necessarily involved the answers to the latter. ... The mystery of homosexuality is therefore by no means so simple as it is commonly depicted in popular expositions—"a feminine mind, bound therefore to love a man, but unhappily attached to a masculine body; a masculine mind, irresistibly attracted by women, but, alas! imprisoned in a feminine body". It is instead a question of three sets of characteristics, namely:
>
> - Physical sexual characteristics (physical hermaphroditism).
> - Mental sexual characteristics (masculine or feminine attitude).
> - Kind of object-choice.
>
> (Freud, 1920a, p. 170)

Freud's distinctions in this paper are crucially relevant to current discussions in the psychoanalytic literature on the relationship between sexuality (as unconscious desire) and gender.

The paper concludes with this well-known reflection:

> psycho-analysis cannot elucidate the intrinsic nature of what in conventional or in biological phraseology is termed "masculine" and "feminine": it simply takes over the two concepts and makes them the foundation of its work. When we attempt to reduce them further, we find masculinity vanishing into activity and femininity into passivity, and that does not tell us enough.
>
> (Freud, 1920a, p. 171)

"A Child Is Being Beaten" (1919e)

"A Child Is Being Beaten: A Contribution to the Study of the Genesis of Sexual Perversion" contains an important discussion in relation to bisexuality. If bisexuality is inherent to all human beings, what is it that is repressed in the course of development?

The text appeared in 1919, in a period of transition between Freud's models of the mind. As Catherine Chabert (2005) indicates, the text's intention was to consider the phantasy of "a child is being beaten" as one of the seduction fantasies and, in addition, to describe the paradigmatic developments involved in the production of this phantasy. At the same time, it featured the "infantile" representations of masochism, heralding works still to come before the publication of *Beyond the Pleasure Principle* (1920g) and "The Economic Problem of Masochism" (1924c), thus anticipating the link between love and punishment, excitation and pain.

The phantasy of a child being beaten is composed of three phases: The scene of the first phase appears as "*My father is beating the child*" (a child is being beaten). The second phase, Freud indicates, is unconscious and is a construction of the transference. It appears as "*I* [girl] *am being beaten by my father*", where the author occupies the place of the beaten child of the first scene. The third phase (which is the one that appears first in the analysis) resembles the first. The author of the phantasy again occupies the place of spectator. However, two notable elements differentiate it. The partners have changed: the beaten child of the first phase has been replaced by a multitude of unknown children and the father (the beater) by more distant substitutes. This shift between the scenes is, Chabert suggests, a fundamental movement of the analysis, "a way of opening up positions of identification in movement" between activity and passivity, sadism and masochism, representations and actions (Chabert, 2005).

This text suggests a link between masochism, femininity, and the guilt feelings engendered by incestuous desires towards the father—desires that are repressed and re-constructed in the analytic process.

Is this seduction by the father, however, not a second one, following a first seduction by the mother? The paper was written before Freud's reformulation of his theory of femininity and the discovery of the pre-oedipal phase. The mother is, according to Freud himself, the first seductress. "The first sexual and sexually coloured experiences which a child has in relation to its mother are naturally of a passive character" (Freud, 1931b, p. 236).

If bisexuality is characteristic of both sexes, then what is it that is repressed in the oedipal phase? Freud examines the idea that it is the opposite of each sex that is repressed. But he considers that such a view would be a return to a biologically determined view on sexuality:

> Such a theory as this can only have an intelligible meaning if we assume that a person's sex is to be determined by the formation of his genitals; for otherwise it would not be certain which is a person's stronger sex and we should run the risk of reaching from the results of our enquiry the very fact which has to serve as its point of departure. To put the theory briefly: with men, what is unconscious and repressed can be brought down to feminine instinctual impulses; and conversely with women.
>
> (Freud, 1919e, p. 201)

His second possibility refers to Alfred Adler's "masculine protest" in that "every individual makes efforts not to remain on the inferior 'feminine line [of development]' and struggles towards the 'masculine line', from which satisfaction can alone be derived" (Freud, 1919e, p. 201).

Freud raises questions about this theory, as it would mean that the repressing agency would always be masculine and the repressed element feminine. He considers that the theory of the masculine protest seems to maintain its ground very much better on being tested with regard to the beating phantasies, as in "both boys and girls the beating-phantasy corresponds with a feminine attitude—one, that is, in which the individual is lingering on the 'feminine line'—and both sexes hasten to get free from this attitude by repressing the phantasy" (Freud, 1919e, pp. 202–203).

Freud's reflections turn, however, to his studies on infantile sexuality in order to indicate how active elements are present. He concludes this text by suggesting that it is infantile sexuality that is the motive force in the formation of symptoms; the Oedipus complex is the nuclear complex of neuroses.

The repudiation of femininity

In 1937 Freud concluded that both sexes "repudiate femininity"—a phenomenon that is an essential element of the asymmetry between the sexes. This repudiation is, Freud suggests, the bedrock of psychoanalysis and part of the great riddle of sex (1937c, p. 252). It is part of the domain of what is unanalysable for Freud.

This is a mysterious statement that has been a source of many debates, especially in France. What did Freud mean? Some authors have suggested that the repudiation of femininity is the repudiation of the child's position of passivity in relation to the mother when the infant is so dependent on her. André Green has suggested a distinction between passivity and passivation. The latter represents a position of receptivity in relation to maternal care, which he regards as a crucial requirement in an analytic process: "Now the psychoanalytic cure is not possible without this confident passivation, where the analysand gives himself to the analyst's care" (Green, 1986c, p. 248),[3] in a transformation of the way the baby trusts the mother's care.

One is reminded that, from early on, Freud equated the feminine with the object of psychoanalytic investigations when he stated: "It is to be suspected that the essentially repressed element is always what is feminine" (1950 [1892–1899], p. 251). The rejection of the feminine could thus be understood, ultimately, as the rejection of the very object of psychoanalytic investigation.

In the *Ego and the Id* (1923b) and until *An Outline of Psycho-Analysis* (1940 [1938]), Freud considers the universality of bisexuality and the notion that in each individual one should be able to find both the positive and the negative Oedipus complex.

Sex and gender: anthropology and cultural studies

If from its beginnings psychoanalysis emphasized the notion of bisexuality and was concerned with the enigma of the difference between the sexes, this issue has also been central to social anthropology (Perelberg, 2016a). All societies are faced with the task of differentiating between the identical and the different (Perelberg, 1990a, 1990b, 1997b, 2016e). The division of gender roles according to sex is universal; it is present in all human societies. Making sense of it is a task—perhaps a lifelong one—for each individual.

According to Héritier, the differences between male and female bodies and between their roles in reproduction are at the base of all systems of representation, and especially beliefs about difference, such as hot/cold, dry/humid, high/low, inferior/superior, light/dark, and so forth (Héritier, 2002, 2012, p. 20). Binary systems, she adds, are at the base of universal categorizations. Héritier addresses the universals surrounding the notions of masculine and feminine in a variety of kinship systems, as well as the cultural images that are present in these differentiations. These are constructs of the culture, not biological givens. Héritier suggests that differentiation between masculine and feminine should not be regarded merely as an addition to the three pillars of culture suggested by Lévi-Strauss (1967)—the incest taboo, the sexual division of labour, and a recognized form of sexual union—but as actually lying at the origins of the other three.

The recognition of the differences between the sexes and the generations, as an outcome of the incest taboo, universally marks the passage from nature to culture (Lévi-Strauss, 1967). Each known society attempts, however, to find its own solutions and responses to the fundamental enigma of these differences through the structures of kinship systems and rituals.

An example is that of the *Naven* ritual among the Iatmul people of New Guinea, in which men dress as women and women dress as men. Bateson's analysis of the ceremony is one of the most fascinating illustrations in the anthropological literature of a response that each culture offers to the enigma of the difference between the sexes. In the context of Iatmul society this refers to the question of what is transmitted through the mother's side and what comes from the father, and the origins of the differentiation between masculine and feminine. The Naven ceremonies are performed to celebrate certain acts and achievements of the *laua* (sister's son) by the *wau* (mother's brother) (Perelberg, 2016e).

There is an inherent contradiction in Iatmul society between the nature of an individual's relationship with his mother's clan and the behaviour that is expected from men—that is, the masculine ethos. Two main dichotomies organize social life: the opposition between men and women and that between the individual matrilineal and patrilineal ties. It is through these contradictions that Bateson analyses the Naven, particularly the transvestism and pantomime that it involves (Bateson, 1936; Perelberg, 2016a).

As far as the distinction between the sexes is concerned, Bateson (1936) indicates that men put an "emphasis and value … upon pride, self-assertion, harshness and spectacular display" (p. 198). They are occupied with violent activities. There is a tendency to histrionic behaviour that transforms harshness into irony, which can turn into buffoonery. The women have a less consistent ethos as, according to Bateson, their lives are more geared towards getting food, rearing children, and "reality". "The normal life of Iatmul women is quiet and unostentatious, while that of men is noisy and ostentatious" (p. 201). In the ceremonial house men display their skills in oratory and in the spectacular; the tone of the debates is, according to Bateson, noisy, angry, and ironical.

Bateson suggests that the difference between the sexes should be understood as being acquired through learning and imitation. In the Naven ceremony, the exaggerated elements of the *wau's* behaviour reflect patterns of behaviour accepted among ordinary Iatmul men.

In a different context, in the annual Brazilian Carnival rituals, men dance and parade in the *Escolas de Samba* dressed as women in ways that at times parody or are a caricature of women. These are just a couple of examples of the way in which the enigma of the difference between the sexes permeates different times, spaces, and cultures. If sexual difference "means no more than one sex is not another" (Mitchell, 2015, p. 84), might one see the infinite variation of expressions of gender identifications in contemporary societies also as attempted answers to the mystery of this basic difference?

If the responses to the enigma of difference between the sexes vary from culture to culture, what is constant and universal, according to Héritier, is inequality between the sexes across cultures. She quotes from a 1995 United Nations Report, which states that full equality between men and women is not to be found in any society (Héritier, 2012). Feminist writers, activists, academics, and clinicians have amply addressed this issue in extremely important ways.[4]

Reading Héritier's texts reminds me of what I wrote in 1990, in *Gender and Power in Families*:

> Gender differences are culturally selected from among biological characteristics and are turned into "natural differences" between the sexes (La Fontaine, 1985). What Westerners regard as the natural characteristics of men and women are neither universal nor natural. The literature abounds with examples which illustrate the variation in these "natural" characteristics. There are parts of New Guinea, for instance, in which men are prudish and flirtatious, preoccupied with cosmetics and their appearance, while women take the initiative in courtship (Mead, 1935; Rosaldo & Lamphere, 1974).
>
> (Perelberg, 1990a, pp. 42–43)

The terms "man" and "woman" are therefore social constructs that legitimize patterns of behaviour (La Fontaine, 1981). However, most societies—whatever their kinship organization or mode of subsistence—tend to give authority and value to the role and activities of men. The diversity in the relationship between the genders is tempered by a common factor of subordination. I have suggested that the universal subordination of women across cultures may be understood as a way in which societies have tried to control the unconscious fears of the all-powerful primitive maternal imago (Perelberg, 2008b, p. 22).

In terms of the framework that is outlined in this chapter, one must also consider Freud's notion of the universality of the (unconscious) repudiation of femininity as the universal signifier of a lack and incompleteness.

The term "gender" was introduced into psychotherapy by the sexologist John Money (Money, Hampson, & Hampson, 1955) and was then taken up by Robert J. Stoller (1968), who coined the term "core gender identity". He introduced the term "gender identity" at the IPA Congress in Stockholm in 1963 (Haraway, 1991, p. 133). Stoller was one of the first clinicians to listen to transsexuals. He put forward a definition of gender that is linked to a biological conception, and he linked sexuality to procreation (Stoller, 1968, p. 4). He suggests, nevertheless, a distinction between sex—as determined by biology—and gender, a term that is psychological or cultural (p. 9). He also integrated the importance of the mother's desire for the establishment of gender into his conceptual framework.

In recent decades, culturalist and constructivist perspectives have had an important impact, especially in academia. Authors such as Butler (1990, 1993), Benjamin (1998), and Harris (2005) have argued for the sociocultural dimensions of gender and identity (Perelberg, 2004b). Butler examines the way in which the apparent unity of biological sex is constructed through discourse and social practices. Benjamin focuses on the way gender is culturally and historically formed in an attempt to de-essentialize gender.

Cyborgs and the pharmacopornographic era

In the 1950s John Money, an endocrinologist from Johns Hopkins Medical School's Gender Identity Clinic, and a colleague, Anke Ehrhardt, inaugurated a research project into sex/gender and developed therapeutic protocols that included surgery, counselling, intervention by social services, and so on. Their book *Man and Woman, Boy and Girl* (Money & Ehrhardt, 1972) became a well-known textbook (in Haraway, 1991, p. 133). This was part of the liberalism in post-Second-World-War Western societies in which the second wave of feminists critiqued the binary oppositions that prevailed in sociology and anthropology (Haraway, 1991, p. 134).

The whole discussion of the area of sex and gender exploded in the US sociological and psychological literature in the 1970s and 1980s. Comparing entries of the word "gender" as a keyword in papers published in *Sociological Abstracts,* Haraway identifies no publications between 1966 and 1970 and 724 entries between 1981 and 1985 (1991, p. 136). The framework of many discussions is to emphasize the primacy of the culture–gender distinction over that between biology and sex.

In 1983 Haraway published the *Cyborg Manifesto* (Haraway, 1991). The cyborg is a hybrid creature, part organism and part machine, partly real, partly fiction—a creature that is present in science fiction films as well as in medicine and is developed also in the context of military defence systems. The term was coined in 1960 by Nathan S. Kline and Manfred Clynes (Kline & Clynes, 1961).[5] This is the inauguration of a world in which the dichotomy between nature and culture, humans and objects would no longer appear to offer a framework for understanding the world, because of the penetration of technology into the human body. The cyborg exists in "a post-gender world" (Haraway, 1991, p. 150); it is devoid of gender, a world without parents who generate the individual (pp. 150–151). In this world the boundaries between human and animal, animal and machine, and the physical and non-physical worlds are blurred (pp. 150–154).

Haraway elaborates a series of oppositions that characterize this development: for example, reproduction is replaced by replication, sex by genetic engineering, labour by robotics, mind by artificial intelligence, and the sequel to the Second World War is Star Wars (pp. 161–162). The dichotomies between mind and body, animals and humans, organism and machine, men and women are called into question (p. 163) and do not constitute a framework for understanding the contemporary world.

In her recent fieldwork in Rio de Janeiro, the anthropologist Silvia Naidin studied the way in which the female sexual body is created via different techniques in different social groups (Naidin, 2013, 2016). This process exists within a technological market that inserted itself in the production of the human sexual body. Obviously, techniques that are aimed at making human bodies more beautiful and desirable through painting and piercing are not new; they have existed perhaps as long as humanity itself. One example that comes to mind is the way in which lips have been enhanced through the use of labrets among tribes in Africa and Amazonia. In Africa, a lower lip plate is usually combined with the excision of the two lower—and sometimes all four—front teeth. Among the Sara and Lobi peoples of Burkina Faso, a plate is also inserted into the upper lip. Other tribes, such as the Makonde of Tanzania and Mozambique, used to wear a plate in the upper lip only. Many older sources reported that in some tribes the plate's size was a sign of social or economic importance.

The fundamental difference, as expressed by so many authors writing about contemporary capitalist societies, is the extent to which technology has penetrated the human body worldwide. If Foucault's writings were ground-breaking in indicating the control that society has exercised over the body, it now seems that a further step has been taken in that the new technologies and new form of capitalism are taking over the *production* of the body itself.

Preciado (2013) coined the term *pharmacopornographic era* to describe the way the pharmaceutical and pornography industries, and late capitalism, are integrated in their responsibility for the regulation of the cycles of reproductive and social control of the human body. Preciado states that the political and technological management of the body and sexuality is a major twenty-first-century industry.[6]

Preciado describes the changes in capitalism whereby gender, sex, sexuality, and sexual identity become "objects of the political management of living" (p. 25).[7] He considers that all these have led to a psychotropic and punk capitalism (p. 33) that has placed the body and sexuality at the centre of an international multimillion-dollar industry: over 1.5 million websites available to adults anywhere (pp. 28–37). This inaugurates capitalism's capacity, in the words of Bruno Latour, to have "material authority" (p. 34). The power of pharmacopornography is to transform depression into Prozac, masculinity into testosterone, and erection into Viagra (p. 34). He thus suggests that contemporary society is inhabited by toxicopornographic subjectivities: "There is nothing to discover in sex or in sexual identity; there is no *inside*" (p. 35). Sex becomes "sex design"; pharmacopornographic industry invents the subject (p. 36) and makes it impossible to think about the demand for a fabricated body outside the context of the current technological framework of contemporary post-imperialist society. The penetration of the body is the outcome of an entire industry (Preciado, 2008, p. 32).[8]

Naidin identified a correlation between *body design* and *social class* in Rio de Janeiro (2016). For the upper middle classes, any aesthetic surgical intervention should enable the individual to look as natural as possible—as if "one had had a good night's sleep". For the lower classes in Rio de Janeiro, in contrast, the demand for bigger bottoms or breasts has given rise to images of bodies that may look like caricatures of the feminine or the masculine, at times blurring these distinctions. The aim of the surgery for a category that she identified as "*supergostosas*" (super-delicious) that submit themselves to surgery to increase bottoms, breasts, or thighs is to create what has been designated "hyperfemininity", which, at times, blends with masculinity. These are hybrid images that blur the distinctions between masculine and feminine. Naidin's fieldwork in Rio de Janeiro enables her to understand that such investment in a specific feminine type of body by the lower classes demands constant, continuous effort and repeated hormone injections, facilitated and stimulated by the pharmaceutical industry.

She gives, as an example, the monologue by Agrado, the transvestite in the 1999 film *All About My Mother*, directed by Pedro Almodóvar:

> As well as being pleasant, I am very authentic. Look at my body! It is made to measure. Eyes in the shape of almonds, 80 thousand. Nose, 200 thousand. … Breasts, two as I am no monster, 70 thousand each. … Silicone? In the lips, front, cheeks, hips and bottom. A litre (of silicone) costs more than 100,000. … Well, as I was saying, it costs a lot to be authentic, ma'am. And one can't be stingy with these things because you are more authentic the more you resemble what you've dreamed of being.
>
> (translated by the author)

Sex, gender and sexuality

I would like to offer the following definitions in order to map the subject under discussion:

Sex refers to a biological differentiation at the base of the cultural attribution of gender roles.

Gender has been defined as a "system of social, symbolic and psychic relations, in which men and women are differently positioned" (Haraway, 1991, p. 143). It is a social construct.

Sexuality refers to unconscious phantasies present in the life of each individual. Sexuality is to do with desire, which is, by definition, perverse and polymorphous, excessive, disruptive, anxiety-provoking, and always in conflict with prohibition and the law against incest.

The object of psychoanalysis is not gender but sexuality, which establishes a link between the sexual and the unconscious. Some crucial concepts that enable us to map sexuality and the unconscious are: the mirror stage, the structuring function of the phallus, castration, desire, *jouissance*, the role of the other in the constitution of the psyche, and the Oedipus complex (Perelberg, 2016b, 2016c). The "unconscious never ceases to challenge our apparent unity as subjects" (Rose, 1982, p. 30). This unity is *specular*, in the words of Lacan—a construction that enables the individual to enter into the realm of symbolic exchanges.

The whole process takes place in an imaginary dimension: the recognition of the self takes place through an optical image and subjective alienation. In Joel Dor's words:

> Although the mirror phase symbolizes the "preformation" of the "I" it presupposes by its fundamental nature the destiny of the "I" as alienated in the imaginary dimension. The re-cognition of the self in the mirror image is accomplished—for optical reasons—through indications that are exterior and symmetrically inserted. … This implies the re-cognition, the alienation and the "beginnings of the chronic misrecognition that will characterize all his future relations with himself".
>
> (Dor, 1998, p. 97)

The I and the body image are thus realized in an alienating process that takes place through the mediation of the other. It is an outcome of the desire of the (m)Other that invests her child's body. It is the mother who indicates to the child that what he sees in the mirror is himself. This will underline how little access the individual has to the reality of his own body. The mother invests the development of her baby's body, admiring, caressing, stroking, dressing her baby, and the way in which she handles this bodily care and development will have an impact on the future of her child's self and other representations. Her own unconscious relationship to her own body and sexuality will have an impact on her child, as discussed by many French analysts (Braunschweig & Fain, 1975; Lacan, 1973; Laplanche, 1987). The child's body image is rooted in the way it is seen and invested by the demand of the

Other. This is at the core of Rimbaud's famous quotation "I is another"—"*Je est un autre*" (letter to Georges Izambard, 13 May 1871, in Harmann, 1958).

The concept of *jouissance* becomes central in this process. *Jouissance beyond the pleasure principle* is opposed to desire *within the pleasure principle*, which is the phallic system. This is in opposition, for example, to psychotic *jouissance*, which remains outside the symbolic realm. The psychotic subject remains outside the "oedipal–phallic protection" (Verhaeghe, 2001, p. 89). The best example is that of Schreber, who believed himself to be a woman and submitted to God's total enjoyment[9] (p. 89).

In psychoanalytic terms, sexual difference is organized around castration, which inserts the individual in a specific position in the oedipal triangle (Mitchell, 1999). This division is eminently symbolic, so that the phallus can be seen as missing in the girl only in terms of a "pre-existing hierarchy of values" (Rose, 1982, p. 43), as "there is nothing missing in the real" (Lacan, 1968, p. 113). Castration becomes the signifier of a dialectic relationship in sexuality; it requires the renunciation of incestuous desires and the inauguration of culture. It is indissolubly linked to the Oedipus complex. In the structural model of the mind this threat is internalized, and the fear of the father becomes the fear of one's own superego. "The selection of the phallus as the mark around which subjectivity and sexuality are constructed reveals, precisely, that they are constructed, in a division that is both arbitrary and alienating" (Mitchell, 1984, p. 256).

However, a child may discover that a woman does not have a penis and yet continue to assume that the mother possesses a phallus. The observation of the anatomical difference is not enough for the registration of this difference. Another aspect will need to be added, which is the threat of castration (Freud, 1924d, p. 252).

Morel provides the following example of a child's resistance to acknowledging the differentiation between the sexes:

> Sara, aged six, a little girl who was in analysis, knew perfectly well, and had evidence to prove it, that boys have a "willy" and girls do not. But she was reticent about it, and immediately afterwards would draw three types of human beings: boys, girls and witches. The last were wearing very tall hats. … Alongside

> "scientific" knowledge with respect to anatomical difference, the unconscious belief in the mother's phallic power remained unaltered.
>
> (Morel, 2011, pp. 77–78)

From my own practice, another example:

> Sam, aged 3, made the following statement: "When I grow up, I want to be a Daddy. Then I will grow up and I will be a Mummy."

The horror of castration is expressed in the notion of the uncanny: something that is at once familiar and yet disturbing (Freud, 1919h). *Unheimlich* (the uncanny) has been interpreted, with reference to the maternal body, to the female maternal organ that has been repressed—something that is known and not known at the same time, a sense of "*déjà vu*" and is nevertheless repressed. (These ideas are developed more fully in the last part of this book.)

In their discussion with Butler, both Mitchell and Rose (Butler, 2015; Mitchell, 2015) emphasize the fundamental principle of sexual difference within the law within a culture that prohibits incest and murder. This is an irreducible principle in psychoanalysis and is to be distinguished from the variations of sexual desire.

Freud pointed out that fluidity that is the hallmark of identificatory processes. This fluidity contrasts with the individual quest for a *coherent* identity, a sense of cohesiveness that is denied him by the very nature of the psychic apparatus.

Laplanche has coined the term "*le sexuel*"—by definition multiple and polymorphous—which refers to infantile, perverse sexuality. He stresses that the "*sexuel*" is the psychoanalytic object (2007):

> The infantile sexuel, the "sexual," is the very object of psychoanalysis. A matter of drives and not instinct, functioning according to a specific economic system that is the seeking of tension and not the seeking of tension reduction, having at its origin the fantasmatic object, at its origin and not at its outcome, hence reversing the "object relation," it comes to take up all the room by trying to organize itself in a way that is always precarious,

> until the upheaval of puberty when the instinctive genital will have to come to terms with it.
>
> (Laplanche, 2007, p. 218)

Laplanche argues that the introduction of the term "gender" into psychoanalysis colludes with those who want to diminish the impact of the Freudian discovery.

The term *sexuation*, as distinct from biological sexuality, has also been coined to designate the way in which the subject is inscribed in the difference between the sexes, specifically in terms of the unconscious and castration—that is, as "inhabiting language" (Lacan, 1998, p. 80). The process of sexuation passes through what comes from the discourse of the other. For Lacan there is a fundamental, specular, imaginary aspect to this.

Some clinical accounts on transsexuals

A few psychoanalysts have written over the years on patients who presented themselves in analysis as transsexuals. Some examples have been discussed by Fairbairn (1931), Stoller (1968), Colette Chiland (2005), Ruth Stein (1995), and Alessandra Lemma (2016).

In 1931 Fairbairn published one of the earliest analyses of a patient who was concerned about her "real" sex. She had been in analysis for nine years. The patient had been depressed, which had led her to stop teaching, but she also had doubts about her "real" sex. At puberty, she was found to have a genital abnormality: she did not menstruate, and her growth was abnormal. When she was 20 years old, it was revealed that she had a complete absence of all genital organs; she had only a very minuscule vagina that "led nowhere" (Fairbairn, 1931, p. 197), and she had no uterus. Later examinations by a gynaecologist concluded that "we are dealing with a condition of essential masculinity with the presence of male gonads accompanied by secondary characters of a female type, that is, which usually goes by the nature of 'male pseudohermaphroditism'" (as reported by the gynaecologist, in Fairbairn, 1931, p. 198). The geneticist whose examination found the presence of female secretory gonads had a different view (p. 198). Although the patient had been a tomboy in her childhood, she had always been attracted to boys and had never had any doubts about her femininity. When she started to work as a teacher, she became too harsh with the children she taught—an expression of a tyrannical superego that demanded perfection. She alternated between periods of mania and of depression.

Her mother had been an energetic person and her father insignificant and passive. The authority in the family resided in her maternal grandfather, who had died a year before the patient started her analysis.

Initially the patient responded well to the analysis with Fairbairn and had an awakening of her sexuality. A period of excitement surrounding this sexual awakening was followed by increased anxiety in relation to men. Fairbairn understood this as her penis envy, oral–sadistic in quality, which provoked enormous unconscious guilt in the patient. The analyst focused his interpretations on the patient's sadism. Morel (2011) indicates that "penis envy was not theorized as a symbolic lack but, rather, as the very concrete envy of, and desire for, an object, like a chocolate she had wanted to steal from the fridge" (p. 170). She emphasizes that Fairbairn's technique "consisted in making his patient feel guilty about her immoral desires". Lacan wondered whether the analyst's technique could have led to a "paranoidization of hysteria" (1991, p. 272).

Morel goes through the details of the case and identifies how, as a child, the patient had had a masculine identification:

> In her imagination she was a man, and the depression she experienced at the time of her "adventures" can be explained by the fact that, when confronted by a man, her narcissistic image, her masculine ego was snatched away. … The analysis should have enabled her to elaborate her castration complex and helped her to assume her privation (the real lack of the symbolic object, the phallus). … Fairbairn, by interpreting the desire for a penis as if it was the desire for a real object, could not allow her to go beyond Penisneid.
>
> (Morel, 2011, p. 172)

Moreover, by concentrating the analysis on the mother–daughter relationship and forgetting about the father, the latter was eliminated in analysis. Hysteria, however, is, as we have also discussed in relation to the case of Dora, "dedicated to exposing the father's impotence" (Freud, 1905e, p. 47).

The subject of the unconscious can be identified only in the context of an analysis. The biological abnormalities in Fairbairn's classical psychoanalytic case did not determine the choice of the process of sexuation.

Stoller was one of the first psychoanalysts to listen to transsexual people and to attempt an outline of the aetiological characteristics of the transsexual. He stressed the importance of differentiating the "true" transsexual from fetishistic cross-dressers, homosexuals, and the psychotic.

Stoller (1968, 1975) underlined the primary importance of the family constellation of the future transsexual. He believed that the mother of the transsexual male boy displayed feelings of deprivation and worthlessness as a female and used this son as her penis—the perfect phallus—that she had always wanted (1975, p. 37). He believes that the only penis such a woman can stand is "a ruined one: beautiful, graceful, but without 'masculine' attributes of dirty, brutal, penetrating sexuality". According to Stoller, the transsexual boy's mother is a woman who, in childhood, develops a strong sense of masculinity that is interwoven with her femininity. These two factors (her bisexuality and depression) compel this type of mother to overwhelm her infant son forcefully and continuously with her presence, from birth until the symbiosis is prised apart by the child going to school, or by treatment (p. 40). In the transsexual, mother and infant remain bound together in a state of blissful symbiosis (p. 45).

The transsexual boy begins to show his extreme femininity by the age of 2–3 years, though first signs may appear as early as the age of 1. Stoller believes that in the earliest stages these boys do not seek femininity but, rather, receive it passively via excessive impingement of the too-loving bodies of their mothers (1975, p. 54).

Stoller distinguishes between transsexual belief and psychotic delusion. He points out that the transsexual realistic assessment of his anatomy is different from the psychotic, who may *literally* believe that his male body has *become* female (Schreber). There is a *knowledge* that the individual belongs to the male sex, but a feeling of somehow *being* of the other sex (p. 77). The feeling of being profoundly feminine coexists with the awareness of the fact of being male (p. 86).

Stoller underscores an important aspect in some of the patients, which is a sense of emptiness. He understands this as the outcome of the mother's inability to transmit to the child that they have a being of their own. Most transsexuals present a great façade, like models and beautiful actresses. The stress on the element of appearance was underpinned subsequently by many authors, like Morel and Lemma (see below).

Stoller indicates that in the transference, the experience of the analyst is that the relationship "does not go anywhere, it has no melody or rhythm, in which the patient demands little from us as humans but rather from us as fixers and soothers" (1975, pp, 113–114). Stoller also insists on the absence of oedipal conflict in transsexuals: however, one of the main aspects that he emphasizes is that the transsexual has no interest in his own penis. A crucial measure as to whether someone is transsexual will be whether he enjoys using his penis for sexual pleasure: this, he will suggest, will constitute a major recommendation against an operation to amputate a penis (p. 253).

He also indicates that some transsexuals have rare orgasms or none. It is specifically around the experience and the uses of the penis that fetishist, transsexual, and homosexual cross-dressing can be differentiated from each other.

Stoller distinguishes between the following:

> (1) *Fetishism*: cross-dressing is not found in transsexuals and is rare in homosexuals; (2) *Erotic pleasure in the penis*: is not present in the transsexual; (3) *Object choice*: the fetishistic cross-dresser ... prefers a female (and experiences himself to be a heterosexual); the homosexual object choice is a male (and senses himself to be homosexual); the male transsexual object choice is a male (and considers himself to be psychologically heterosexual but anatomically "homosexual"); (4) *Sense of maleness:* the fetishistic cross-dresser values his penis, his maleness and his masculinity; the same is true of the homosexual; the transsexual cannot stand his maleness or his genitals and makes tremendous efforts to get rid of them.
>
> (Stoller, 1975, p. 156)

Stoller nevertheless acknowledges that there are patients who do not fit into any of these groups.

Following Fairbairn, MacAlpine, Hunter, Searles, and White, Stoller points out the regression towards merging with a primitive mother. He believes that he is identifying a more primitive process in that this merger is not a defensive process (p. 289).

On the basis of substantial clinical experience at the Portman Clinic, Limentani (1979) shares some of the ideas developed by Stoller: he also understands transsexualism to develop against the background of profound early disturbance of symbol formation arising from the fantasy of fusion between mother and child. This is aggravated by the absence of a paternal influence. Limentani believes, however, that transsexuality is defensive against a particularly threatening type of separation anxiety that is common to both sexes. Transsexualism in some cases appears to be the precursor of transvestism or homosexuality.

Oppenheimer (1991) has criticized Stoller's views as "objectifying" the subject's manifest claim to have a woman's soul in a man's body—stripping the drive from its understanding, as the transsexual strips it from his life. For him, transsexualism is associated with the narcissistic pathology defined by Kohut (1977, 1984) as a lack of structuring of the self, which is weak, deficient, or disturbed, accompanied by a secondary structural formation connected with this first defect (Oppenheimer, 1991, p. 228). The transsexual subject possesses the narcissistic characteristics of low self-regard, negative self-representation, and alternation of self states; his disturbance involves a particular more or less unknown sector of the self: sexuality. For Oppenheimer, the "fixation on femininity" makes sense only "by deferred action"—it is recathected as a compensation for and defence against the trauma represented by the lack of the father and the excess of the mother's presence. The father's absence also proves to be traumatic "by deferred action".

Ruth Stein (1995) understands her male patient's wish to become a woman, to be a transsexual in a literal meaning of the word:

> the analysis revealed that, it was not "womanization" or "feminization" the patient sought, but "transsexualism", i.e. "transcending the sexual barrier, tearing down the constraints of biological sex that limit every human being". In his omnipotent, superior state of mind, he desired not only to be a "better" woman than

> his mother and sister, an ambition he had nurtured in his fantasy, but, ultimately, to be a man and a woman at the same time, not to have to reckon with difference (see Dimen, 1991), and not to have to renounce anything or anybody (see Chasseguet-Smirgel, 1984, and McDougall's, 1986, concept of neo-sexuality)—neither his father nor his mother—and thus not to undergo the pain of mourning". In this case of analysis, the patient did not undergo surgery.
>
> (Stein, 1995, p. 285)

This has points of contact with André Green's conceptualization of the neuter gender.

Quinodoz (1998) took into analysis a man who had undergone a vaginoplasty. She identities a psychotic and a neurotic part of her patient's personality. *On the psychotic level, the delusional neo-reality of the appearance of a woman sought to replace the unbearable reality of being a man, whereas the neurotic part was aware that s/he could never really be a woman.* The author observes that *in this analysand sexualization served to conceal a fundamental narcissistic fault.* She also describes how she worked with her own madness to help the patient emerge from a situation of paradoxical fusion with the mother in madness.

Simone was more like the subjects described by Oppenheimer: her conscious motivation had been hatred of the penis and horror of being a man.

Quinodoz suggests that her patient's vaginoplasty had been a form of "acting out with a sexualizing effect" (as Oppenheimer put it), aiming at "the construction of a neo-reality (the appearance of a woman) in the place of an unbearable reality (being a man), in order to fill a narcissistic fault and perhaps to avoid a delusional breakdown" (p. 104).

In some cases of transsexualism, Morel has suggested, the wish to eliminate the sexual organ is "not requested so that the subject can experience the sexual *jouissance* of the other sex, but rather for reasons of 'being' (appearances, social identity, change of status, etc.)" (Morel, 2011, p. 187; see also Lemma, 2013). Lemma also emphasizes the visual aspect: some transsexuals wish to have an operation to remove their penis in terms of how they look, rather than it being a question of desire. In the case of her patient, Ms A, she observed that "her body felt shut down, turned away from anything alive, like a ghost dressed up with nowhere to go" (p. 281).[10]

István/Steven/Stefánie [Stefi]

Steven was already in his mid-70s when he decided to take the ultimate step and undergo an operation to transition from male to female. In the early years of the twenty-first century he travelled to Thailand, where the operation was much more affordable.

Born in Hungary in the late 1920s, the son of a well to do Jewish family, he was called István. The parents had lost twin sons soon after birth prior to having him, under circumstances that never became clear. One can imagine that some of the distance that the parents kept in relation to their next-born might have been connected with a melancholic state, the outcome of these great losses. His mother was said to be a narcissistic woman, greatly concerned with her appearance. She thought that her son looked like a weakling (Faludi, 2017, p. 126). The father was described within the family as weak and ineffectual. As he was growing up, István had many comforts (nannies, teachers, toys), but not his parents' presence. The couple often travelled, and the child István was left behind.

The parents separated when he was 12, accusing each other of having affairs. The father had, on occasion, asked the son to spy on his mother for him. Undecided about who he should live with, István went to live with a teacher, although another version of this period of his life was that he was out of control at home, and his parents did not know how to deal with him.

After his parents' separation, István felt depressed. One day he was nearly run over by a tram, when suddenly a hand pulled him out of danger. It was his father's—"my guardian angel", Stefánie said later (p. 127). When he turned 13, his father gave him a movie camera, as well as (he later found out) a prayer book, but neither his father nor his mother attended his Bar-Mitzvah. This movie camera became a major companion in his life.

After the war, István set out with the Danish Red Cross, which took him and a friend to Vienna, and then to Copenhagen. From Copenhagen, thanks to a fake passport and documents, he managed to travel to Brazil, where, together with two Hungarian friends, he spent five years working for the geographic institute, and he made a name for himself as a photographer through his documentaries and the photographs that he took all over the country (p. 313). As a professional photographer, his speciality was montage and photographic manipulation. After five years in Brazil, he travelled to the United States to re-find a girl with whom he had been infatuated.

As a man, István engaged in many kinds of sports—running, mountaineering, rock climbing, sailing—and he had also been an explorer in the forests of Brazil. Sexually he had always been attracted to women and had had sexual relationships only with women. In the United States he was married and had two children, a girl and a boy, although he himself always experienced himself as distant from both of them.

When, after some 12 years of marriage, István's wife filed for divorce, he fought against it. The period surrounding the divorce gave rise to an uncontrollable rage; there is also at least one earlier example of violence against his daughter, when he banged her head against the floor (p. 284) . Ironically, in terms of what would happen later, the violence of this scene is attributed to her being accused of wanting to leave Judaism behind her. Once he attacked his wife with one of the chairs in the dining room. His wife managed to get a restraining order, which he ignored. He defied one restraining order after another. There was an episode of extreme violence against his ex-wife's lover, which led the ex-lover to break the door of the marital home with a baseball bat. Steven ended up stabbing this man with a Swiss Army knife (p. 417). He was arrested, and the so-called intruder—his wife's lover—was taken to hospital. He himself had minor injuries and spent the night in prison. He nevertheless managed to persuade the police that he had been the wronged husband, defending his family. After the divorce, distancing himself from Judaism, Steven became a devote of televangelism—evangelic services via television programmes (p. 271).

He returned to Hungary and was then estranged from the whole family for some 25 years; he then contacted his daughter again, letting her know that she had transitioned into a woman, writing: "I have had enough of impersonating a macho aggressive man that I have never been inside."

In the years before he transitioned, he liked to insert pictures of him/herself into internet images displayed by magazines such as

Vogue or *Brides*. For instance, there was an image of himself over a woman ironing lingerie, or an online Christmas card of a girl wearing a red frill around her neck, but otherwise naked. He also liked to visit FictionMania, a large transgender website that showed thousands of stories and pictures of "forced feminisation fiction". "You know", he would tell his daughter many years later, "stories … like they're little boys and their mothers make them dress up as a girl as punishment and their mothers spank them" (p. 73). He had a penchant for stories of subjugation and domestic service set in Victorian times.

All this, he would later explain, was before he became a "real woman".

Once, after the operation, Stefi said:

> I had the organs, I did my job, as a man. But I didn't fit the role. They didn't approve of me. … Women didn't approve of me. I didn't know how to fight and get dirty. I am not muscular, I am not athletic, I had a miserable life as a man. … Now, as a woman, women like me more. I fit my role better as a woman than when I was miscast in the wrong role. … Now I am completely like a woman. … You have to get rid of old habits. If you don't, you're going to be like a stranger all the time, with this … *this anxiety of non-belonging.*
>
> (Faludi, 2017, pp. 95–96)

Stefánie had been the photographer Steven Faludi before he transitioned, and István Friedman in his native country of Hungary. His story is seen through the lens of his daughter, Susan Faludi, in her marvellous book *In the Dark Room* (2017), from which all the information above is quoted.[11] She traces István's story through her interviews with him, inserting her narrative within a harrowing account of extreme anti-Semitism in twentieth-century Hungary, anti-Semitism that preceded the Holocaust.

At the time of the First World War, Hungarian Jews went from being among the most assimilated in Europe to being the target of extreme anti-Semitic legislation of the new century. By the late 1930s, all of their property had been confiscated, and they were forbidden access to their own professions and denied their rights as citizens. Nearly half a million Hungarian Jews would be sent to be murdered in Auschwitz.

During the war, the family property was seized. István, as an adolescent, seemed to have spent a great deal of the war struggling on his own, moving from hiding place to hiding place. He did not stay in the designated places for Jews, from where most were deported; eventually, via one of the Zionist underground movements, he managed to get for himself an armband of one of the Hungarian Nazi-aligned parties (Faludi, 2017, p. 249). At that time, some Jews who had not been deported were restricted to certain "protected houses", where more than 40 people could be confined in one room. These were houses along the river near St Stephen's Park, where Jews had been taken after Sweden, Switzerland, Portugal, Spain, and the Vatican started to issue tens of thousands of safe-conduct passports in an attempt to shield the city's Jews from deportation (p. 249). Armed gangs of Arrow Cross adherents would invade the protected houses, take the Jews away, torture them, and shoot them, throwing the bodies into the Danube. "To save on bullets Arrow Cross gunmen tied people together—often family members—shot one into the river, and let the sinking corpse drown the rest" (p. 250).

By 1944, István's parents were in one of these protected houses. One day István showed up; impersonating a Nazi soldier wearing a Hungarian Nazi armband, he presented himself to the guards with a rifle, and told them that he had orders to take the Friedmans away. He thus saved them. They survived the war hidden in the flat of a neighbour who was a doctor. In 1946 the Friedmans became the Faludis—an old Magyar name, meaning "of the village" (p. 65).

After the war, István's parents emigrated to Israel, where they eventually died. In spite of his mother constantly writing to him and asking him to write back to her, he refused further contact with his parents.

Reflecting on her father's transition, Susan Faludi examines the context of extreme anti-Semitism in twentieth-century Hungary. Jewish men were seen as effeminate and not as proper men.

> Jewish men were said to be plagued by the female ailments of hysteria and neurasthenia, prone to fainting spells and tubercular pallor... lacking in reproductive vigour, afflicted with venereal disease, and beset by sexual "abnormalities" of an effeminate and submissive nature.
>
> (Faludi, 2017, pp. 276–277)

Jewish men considered dangerous precisely because their weakness required them to prey on the vitality of healthier races (p. 280). In Hungary, by conflating effeminacy and aggression through the body of the Jewish man, blood libel served as a linchpin between religious hatred and sexual phobia (p. 280).

Faludi quotes Ander Gilman: "Modern Jewishness became as much a category of gender as race" (p. 281).

Although Susan Faludi in no way attempts to explain Steven's transition into Stefi only in terms of this extremely anti-Semitic, hostile environment, she also suggests that this cannot not be taken into account. Was her father's transition an attempt to eradicate the figure of the Jewish man and transform himself into a non-Jewish woman? Although his Judaism would also emerge at various points in the time they were to spend together, such as when they were in the flat—now being used as a synagogue—where István had hidden with his own father during the war. In one of their conversations, Stefi said:

> They see you as some sort of monster. They don't know what you do. You're vermin. They gas you.
>
> I am accepted better now as a woman than I ever was as a man. (p. 283)

Susan Faludi's thinking is subtle and sophisticated:

> As I confronted, nearly three decades and nine ones away, my father's new self, it was hard for me to purge that image of the violent man from her new persona. Was I supposed to believe the one had been erased by the other, as handily as the divorce decree recast my father as the "endangered" victim? Could a new identity not only redeem but expunge the predecessor? (p. 56)

Was Stefi's transitioning an attempt to create a new persona and leave behind someone that she felt was despised? Could one separate the wish to leave behind her violent self as a man from her wish to leave behind the despised Jew? One's attention is also drawn to the lack of erotic investment in the young István by his parents. He seems to have grown up in an environment of parental indifference, with absent and depriving parents. What comes across in his daughter's account is the lack of eroticism and desire in the wish to "become a woman", and the emphasis on clothes, make-up, appearance. Susan Faludi describes the way Stefi wanted to be seen as a woman in the glimpses she would offer of her underwear, the intimate pieces of clothing, especially when Susan first started to visit her in Hungary. The brief reference to dressing in his mother's clothes reminds me of some patients' accounts in the consulting room, where this becomes a way of having intimate contact with the body of the mother, at times a phantasy of being the mother herself.

Susan Faludi studies the first wave of the literature of transgender individuals that take the shape of memoirs. These tend to emphasize a narrative of transformation from the person who previously existed to a new persona (pp. 153–156). She does not feel pressurized to affirm that her father had got in touch with a true, feminine self that would reveal itself though his surgery. Rather, she believes that Stefi's surgery introduced another layer into a complex psychological structure. "I am a woman—with a birth certificate that says I'm a woman. So I must be a woman" (p. 425), Stefanie asserts.

I found this book particularly moving in terms of Susan's struggle to understand her father. One does not have access to István/Steven/Stefi as one might to a patient's unconscious phantasies in the consulting room, but the contrast between Stefi's visibility and István/Steven's dark room—an image that is over-determined in the book—comes across in powerful ways. One can understand the attempt to create a new persona, separate from previous experiences (see also Sluhovsky, 2017). Might the young István have phantasized not only about being like his mother, as he entered her clothes in her absence, but also about *being* his mother as a young boy? We don't know.

When Susan Faludi discovered one of the documents that her father should have presented before transitioning, the psychologist's opinion was that she was facing a man whereby "a straightforward indication of transsexuality cannot be verified without doubts" (Faludi, 2017, p. 361). It revealed, rather, that her father did not know what he wanted to do or who he wanted to be (p. 361). Her father had not presented this document and had, instead, forged another one, which was accepted in Thailand. His daughter was to write the following:

> And it highlighted the contradictions in a psychology—what transgender writer Sandy Stone would describe as 'the complexities and ambiguities of lived experience'—that my father did not want examined. The larger questions the report raised were the very ones my father hoped to quash with a category-to-be made absolute surgery. The psychologist saw a patient troubled by "disharmony of the desires" whose "impersonal eroticism "was estranged with "feelings of guilt" and whose mental landscape was "impregnated with an uncertainty" that ranged far beyond sexuality and gender. What my father wanted the psychologist to see and validate was a patient whose conflicts were either contained within or irrelevant to a single problem of identity, which could be resolved with a physical solution.
>
> (Faludi, 2017, p. 367)

We know that the newly acquired gender appeared to be the solution for a multitude of conflicts.

In a recent paper Lemma suggests, in the analysis of her patient Celine, who declared herself as "trans" at the beginning of their work together, that the patient was rather lost, confused, and unable to sustain intimate relationships (Lemma, 2016). This is also the case for several of the clinical cases presented in *Psychic Bisexuality: A British–French Dialogue* (Perelberg, 2018b). The individual feels alienated—"neither dead nor alive (Rolland, 2007), caught up in an obsessional doubt, neither yes, nor no" (Green, 1986c, see also Campbell, 2018; Green, 1973), or unable to be either one *or* the other, or one *and* the other (Chabert, 2018). At times these patients attempt to deal with these alienating identifications by establishing a sense of identity, saying "I am this, and not that and not that" (see Campbell, 2018; Chabert, 2018; Zilkha, 2018; see also Perelberg, 1997b, for work with violent patients who attempt to establish a persona through the violent act). One is thus not addressing the choice of the object of desire but, rather, the individual's disturbed relationship to their body and their unconscious identifications. To my way of thinking, the pitfall is, once again, for a conscious discourse to be taken literally.[12]

This demand for an actual change in the body may be understood as the outcome of the foreclosure of the signifier of the phallus. It is an attempt to make a correction in anatomy, whereas the real issue lies at the juncture of the real and the symbolic (Morel,

2011, p. 186). In some of the cases of women wanting to have a penis, something that belongs to the symbolic level (castration) is taken as a concrete reality. In reality, however, there has been no castration![13]

Gozlan suggests that transsexuality can be viewed as a "particular embodiment of sexual difference that captures a universal enigma at the heart of subjectivity" (2015, p. 12). He believes that when gender is conceived as naturally given or, at the other extreme, as "a matter of choice" (Gherovici, 2010), "what gets foreclosed is the incommensurability between the symbolic articulation of gender and the real of sexual difference" (Gozlan, 2015, p. 13). The relationship between the sexed body and gender identity is fragile at best. Psychoanalytic theories move between what Gozlan regards as the "compulsion" to uphold the normative binary gender system and the acknowledgment of the radical heterogeneity of the drive.

Gozlan suggests that the question of transsexual surgery should be understood in terms of "transitioning", not reassignment, and that this opens a new discourse of agency (p. 92). Transsexuality can thus be conceptualized as a signifier for a liminal space that challenges the finitude of gender and calls for a recounting of history—one that is ruptured, opaque and incomplete.[14,15]

I believe that there is, at times, confusion between the patient's conscious discourse and the analyst's interpretations. Rather than attesting to the incompleteness and fragmented, perverse nature of sexuality, the transsexual individual appears, paradoxically, to insist on a clear categorization. Within a psychoanalytic framework, however, we are all bisexual, and there is no definition of an individual's sexuality and desire outside this framework.[16] I wonder whether a distinction between sex, gender, and sexuality might be helpful to firmly remain within an understanding of masculinity and femininity as psychic positions.

In psychoanalysis, taking into account the fluidity of identifications, it is clear that absolute certainty about one's identifications expresses a confusion of registers—addressing as real something that belongs to the symbolic sphere.

Gregorio Kohon (2018) argues that "queer theory has desexualized identity" (p. 268). The concept of sexual difference, a concept specific to psychoanalytic theory, "was expelled from theoretical discourse and reduced to a biological distinction" (p. 268). He argues for the recognition of humans' finitude and acceptance that desires can never be fulfilled. "In sexual difference, there is always something missing" (p. 271). He quotes Mitchell: "because human subjectivity cannot ultimately exist outside a division into one of the two sexes, then it is castration that finally comes to symbolize this split" (Mitchell, 1986, p. 393). Castration conveys, above all, something about the uniqueness of each sex.

In this chapter I am putting forward my view that the object of psychoanalysis is psychosexuality, which is, in the final analysis, determined not by having a male or a female body, but by the unconscious phantasies that are reached *après-coup* through tracing the nuanced interplay of identifications as they are projected, enacted, and experienced in the transference and the countertransference in the analytic encounter. In the words of Rose: "however clear you are in your own mind about being a man or a woman, the unconscious knows better" (Rose, 2016, p. 12).[17]

The paradigmatic example is that of Winnicott, who says to his patient: "I know perfectly well that you are a man but I am listening to a girl, and I am talking to a girl. I am telling this girl: 'You are talking about penis envy'." "If I were to tell someone about this girl", the patient replies, "I would be called mad" (Winnicott, 1971a, p. 73). Winnicott himself, nevertheless, is blurring the distinction between sexuality and gender in this formulation, when he states: "I know perfectly well that you are a man" (see also Richard, 2019).

Sexual difference is the basis of a psychoanalytic understanding of sexuality; it should not be confused with *sexual differences* (Mitchell, 1999, 2015).[18] The former is to do with an organizing principle that indicates that completeness is not possible, that one cannot possess one's mother or kill one's father. It is at the order of the law (Perelberg, 2009b, 2016e, 2018a). The oedipal configuration confronts the child with the fact that they cannot have both sexes and cannot possess either of their parents. The latter—sexual differences—refers to a variety of ways in which individuals decide to practise their sexualities. Sexual difference is inaugurated by the law that prohibits incest and murder, the constitution of the superego and repression. These are the key concepts of a psychoanalytic understanding of sexuality and bisexuality.

Notes

1 Leclaire has suggested that the question of the hysteric is "Am I a man or a woman?" (Leclaire, 1975; see also Kohon, 1986; Lacan, 1981). It is a question of shifting identifications in an attempt to retain one identification, which is phallic. This is also present in some violent patients (Perelberg, 1999a, 1999b).

2 Michel Fain has suggested that sexuality is a constant oscillation between hysteria and orgasm (in Schaeffer, 1986, p. 944).

3 Chasseguet-Smirgel has suggested that femininity stands for receptivity (1964, 1976). M. Eglé Laufer, in numerous published and unpublished papers (e.g., Laufer, 1993), has addressed the active and passive identification and the relationship to the body in adolescence.

4 The legislation about the relationship between men and women in the political and economic sphere attests to the fact that equality between the sexes has not been achieved. Nowadays this has become more complex when considering the slow progress towards achieving full LGBT rights. In 2011, the United Nations Human Rights Council passed its first resolution recognizing LGBT rights, which was followed up with a report from the UN Human Rights Commission documenting violations of the rights of LGBT people, including hate crime, criminalization of homosexuality, and discrimination. The UN Human Rights Commission urged all countries that had not yet done so to enact laws protecting basic LGBT rights. There is huge variation in the recognition of these rights around the world.

5 In the discussions surrounding definitions of the term, it is thought that a human with an artificial cardiac pacemaker or implantable cardioverter-defibrillator would be considered a cyborg, "since these devices measure voltage potentials in the body, perform signal processing, and can deliver electrical stimuli, using this synthetic feedback mechanism to keep that person alive. Implants, especially cochlear implants, that combine mechanical modification with any kind of feedback response are also cyborg enhancements" (https://en.wikipedia.org/wiki/Cyborg).

6 Preciado is currently professor of Political History of the Body, Gender Theory, and History of Performance at Université Paris VIII and is the director of the Independent Studies Program (PEI) of the Museum of Contemporary Art of Barcelona (MACBA). Preciado announced in 2014 that he was transitioning and, in January 2015, changed his first name from *Beatriz* to *Paul*. The book *Testo Junkie: Sex, Drugs, and Biopolitics in the Pharmacopornographic Era* relates Preciado's experience in self-administering testosterone. It was published

in Spain in 2008 (as *Testo yonqui*) and translated into English in 2013. He states: "I'm not taking testosterone to change myself into a man or as a physical strategy of transsexualism; I take it to foil what society wanted to make of me, so that I can write fuck, feel a form of pleasure that is postpornographic ..." (Preciado, 2013, p. 16). He asks: "what kind of feminist am I today: a feminist hooked on testosterone or a transgender body hooked on feminism?" (p. 22).

7 Preciado notes a number of events that led to the progressive creation of this *pharmacopornographic era.* These include: the major investments in the field of sex and sexuality in the United States during the Cold War; the greater visibility and political forms of homosexuality in places such as the US military; the period of McCarthyism, which included the persecution of homosexuals as a form of antinationalism; the establishment of large public health research centres; the first demographic research into sexual deviance undertaken by George Henry and Robert Dickinson; Ray and Charles Eames' collaboration with the US army to construct small boards of moulded plywood to use as splints for army members who had suffered amputations; the beginnings of the commercial use of hormones such as progesterone and oestrogen, and of synthetic molecules (most notably, in 1946, the contraceptive pill), which introduced a radical transformation in the definitions of sexual identities; the introduction of the term "gender" (coined in 1955 by the psychiatrist John Money to indicate the culturally recognized group to which the individual belongs as either masculine of feminine; Money, Hampson, & Hampson, 1955); the beginnings of facelifts and other aesthetic procedures in the United States and Europe (for example, the photographs of Andy Warhol during plastic surgery, transforming his body into an object of consumption). Following the Second World War, de-circumcision—the artificial reconstruction of the prepuce—became one of the most practised surgical operations in the United States. The first transsexual operation on an American soldier took place in 1952, when George W. Jorgensen was transformed into Christine; the creation of *Playboy* magazine; the first phalloplastic surgery, performed in the United Kingdom (between 1946 and 1949) to transform a woman into a man. In 1966 the first antidepressants were created. The first pornographic film, *Deep Throat,* was released in 1972, and it inaugurated a boom in pornographic films. In 1973 homosexuality was withdrawn as a mental illness from the DSM; in 1983 transsexuality was included in the DSM. In 1984 a "sexual pacemaker" was implanted in the penis of a patient, enabling erection by remote control (p. 29). In 1988 Viagra was licenced, to deal with erectile dysfunction (pp. 25–28). The Cold War military technological

explorations were also the "site of production of a new form of technological embodiment" (p. 30) (Preciado, 2013). It was in 1994 that the gene DSS, which is responsible for sexual abnormalities, was discovered. These discoveries have introduced a change in contemporary views on gender.

8 Stryker makes the following statement: "The transsexual body is an unnatural body. It is the product of medical science. It is a technological construction. It is flesh torn apart and sewn together again in a shape other than that in which it was born" (in Rose, 2016). Stryker drew an analogy between herself and Frankenstein.

Susan O'Neal Stryker is an American professor, author, filmmaker, and theorist whose work focuses on gender and human sexuality. She is associate professor of Gender and Women's Studies, director of the Institute for LGBT Studies, and founder of the Transgender Studies Initiative at the University of Arizona. She is the author of several books about LGBT history and culture. She transitioned from being a male to being a female presentation after her doctoral studies (https://en.wikipedia.org/wiki/Susan_Stryker).

9 Schreber believed that he could restore the world to the state of "bliss" (a state of uninterrupted enjoyment; Freud, 1911c, p. 29) "if he were first transformed from a man into a woman" (1911c, p. 16).

10 As Rose describes it: "at the end of her photo session with Annie Leibovitz, Jenner looked at the gold medal she had won as Bruce Jenner in the 1976 Olympic decathlon and commented as 'her eyes rimmed red and her voice grew soft': 'That was a good day. But the last couple of days were better.' It's as if—even allowing for the additional pathos injected by Buzz Bissinger, who wrote the famous piece on Jenner for *Vanity Fair*—the photographic session, rather than hormones or surgery, were the culmination of the process (though Leibovitz herself insists the photos were secondary to the project of helping Caitlyn to 'emerge')" (Rose, 2016).

11 I am grateful to Gregorio Kohon, who first mentioned this book to me.

12 Morel has suggested that Stoller's concept of "gender identity" is based on his theory about the conscious discourse of transsexualism (Morel, 2011, p. 59): "Certainly he is faithful to the clinic of transsexualism, but at the same time his theory of gender identity remains too close to what is said by the subjects he listens to, which is taken almost literally. What they say should rather be elaborated and interpreted in a coherent theory of sexuation" (p. 60).

13 Chiland (2005) views transsexuality as a demand addressed to the Other. The author traces the history of sex change from pagan and early Christian rites to the Skoptzy sect of twentieth-century Russia

that required the severance of the genitals of the new adepts. She believes that male transsexuals seem to identify with the woman, "who replaces the name-of-the-Father" (p. 140). In relation to female transsexuals, Chiland suggests that they fail to identify with The Woman and from that "infer that they cannot be a woman … failing to grasp that the woman's place is to be found at the dehiscence that separates her from The Woman" (p. 140) and thinking, instead: "if not woman, then man" (p. 140). The surgeon and the endocrinologist provide an answer to the question "Am I a man or a woman?" According to Chiland, this, paradoxically, makes the transsexual the object of their desire. The analyst, through not replying to the question, leaves it open.

14 However, as Rose has suggested, "transition does not so much mean crossing from one side to the other as hovering in the space in between, something has to be acknowledged by the watching world (out of an estimated 700,000 trans women and men in the United States, only about a quarter of the trans women have had genital surgery)".

The House of Commons report *Transgender Equality* notes the serious consequences of the high levels of prejudice (including in the provision of public services) experienced by trans people on a daily basis … half of young trans people and a third of adult trans people attempt suicide.

15 Gozlan (2015) suggests that the artists Anish Kapoor and Louise Bourgeois are both preoccupied with the enigma of embodiment and reveal in their work "the precariousness of our signifying categories in the face of the body's inexhaustible inscrutability" (p. 19). He regards Kapoor's abstract sculpture *Memory* as expressing the inherent tension when approaching an enigmatic object. Bourgeois' work captures incoherence, "the borderline zone between being and not-being, separation and joining" (p.19). However, even if he states that transsexuality is a signifier "that takes different meanings at different times" (p. 23), he paradoxically risks reifying the transsexual. In contrast, Juliet Mitchell, in her Foreword to Perelberg's *Psychic Bisexuality* (Mitchell, 2018), refers to Bourgeois as "subjective bisexuality's most profound portraitist". Kohon has argued for the commonality of experience between aesthetics and psychoanalysis and suggests that both art and psychoanalysis must be considered on their own terms (Kohon, 2016).

16 Gherovici (2010) and Verhaeghe (2009) have developed the view that transsexual surgery may be understood as a way of claiming one's desire. I think that at times there is confusion between the literal discourse of the patient and a psychoanalytic understanding of the demand.

Transsexuality, nevertheless, has become a larger topic than it is possible to discuss in the framework of this book. I can only offer a few points of reference for discussion.

17 The degree of legal recognition provided to transgenderism varies widely around the world. Many countries now legally recognize sex reassignments by permitting a change of legal gender on an individual's birth certificate. For instance, in Iran, from the mid-1980s, transgender individuals were officially recognized by the government and allowed to undergo sex reassignment surgery. The government provides up to half the cost for those needing financial assistance, and a sex change is recognised on the birth certificate.

In the United Kingdom, the Gender Recognition Act of 2004 gives people with gender dysphoria legal recognition as members of the sex appropriate to their gender (male or female), allowing them to acquire a new birth certificate and affording them full recognition of their acquired sex in law for all purposes, including marriage. Currently new laws are being debated that would enable an individual to declare their gender, rather than having to undergo surgery. The Republic of Ireland adopted a gender recognition law in 2015, allowing transgender people to change their gender on a self-declaratory basis by filling out a simple form.

www.theguardian.com/commentisfree/2018/oct/17/the-guardian-view-on-the-gender-recognition-act-where-rights-collide

This constitutes an area of political, social, and psychological debate. In 1979 Janice Raymond pronounced in *The Transsexual Empire: The Making of the She-Male* that transgender people are a masculine artefact, another step in the oppression of women. In her view, male-to-female transsexuals should therefore be excluded from women-only spaces.

Jacqueline Rose states at the end of her article (2016): "Arguments about whether trans women and men reinforce or disrupt conventional gender categories, or whether trans women experience themselves the same way as non-trans feminists, are futile. In the complex realm of human sexual life, no one should be deciding these matters for anyone else. You can—we should—liberalise the law on behalf of oppressed groups, but you cannot legislate the unconscious."

18 In the words of Stryker, a "heteroglossic outpouring of gender positions from which to speak" (in Rose, 2016, p. 5).

Part II

EXCESS AND REPRESENTATION

Clinical configurations

2

ON EXCESS, TRAUMA, AND HELPLESSNESS

Repetitions and transformations

Excess—from the Latin *excessus*, from *excedere* "to go out, surpass"—is defined in the *Oxford Dictionary* as "an amount of something that is more than necessary, permitted, or desirable". The notion of an amount implies a quantitative factor not reducible to representation.

The notion of investment lies at the core of Freud's understanding of psychic functioning. From his "Project" (1950 [1895]), written in 1895 but published after his death, to the *Outline of Psychoanalysis* (1940 [1938]), Freud attempts to map the links between the somatic and the psychic. Already in *Studies on Hysteria* (1895d) trauma is conceived of as an overwhelming event that breaches the subject's protective shield, with catastrophic results for the mind. The topographical model of the mind traced the vicissitudes of the relationship between drives and representations; the paradigm for this phase of psychoanalysis was *The Interpretation of Dreams* (1900a), with its distinctions between manifest and latent content and the rules of primary process.

In 1920, however, Freud postulated the existence of a drive that does not correspond to any representation but is expressed through the repetition compulsion (1920g). The structural model of the mind instituted a close relationship between the id and the soma. The id is described as "chaos, a cauldron full of seething excitations" (1933a, p. 73). Psychoanalytic work becomes concerned with how the experience of the infantile traumatic past in its unmetabolizable aspects is repeated in the consulting room. If the drives are at the root of psychic activity, this "implies that something is basically in excess, an overload charge on the mind, linked with the bodily exigencies of the drives whose derivatives have to be sent back to the unconscious because their free expression forbids psychic organisation" (Green, 1998, p. 660).

In a series of papers, Stein (1998, 2008) addresses how the notion of excess is at the core of some major psychoanalytic writings, from Freud to Lacan (1956–60, 1966 [1949]) and Laplanche (1981, 1987, 1999).

In previous writings I have suggested that the notions of "excess" and "emptiness" in the analytic process could be exemplified by contrasting two types of narcissistic configurations (Perelberg, 2003, 2004a). In the first type, intolerance of the other is dealt with by expulsion and violence; in the second, it is dealt with by withdrawal. The example of a patient who has lived through experiences of excess and flooding contrasts with another patient whose narcissism was expressed through withdrawal. They are also profoundly different in terms of what they provoke in the countertransference.[1]

There are patients who fill the consulting room, not only through their emotions and their actions, but also with their words, dreams, and associations. Fundamentally, the feeling one has is as if an excess of representations dominates the consulting room. The experience is that the analyst is overincluded in the patient's world. The patient has dreams that refer directly to the analyst, and one feels constantly overinvolved in his or her analysis. It may seem a paradox to refer to such patients as expressing a lack of a capacity to represent in their way of communicating to the analyst. The notion of "endopsychic perception" is helpful here. Freud has used it in order to refer to the way the mind represents itself unconsciously in dreams and hallucinations (Freud, 1907a). My suggestion is that the excess of representations points to the excess of excitation that is present in the way of relating to the analyst and to their internal objects.

On the other hand, there are patients who create an empty space in the analyst's mind. The response they provoke is a lack of a chain of associations in the analyst, a kind of depressive feeling that remains after they leave. The patient may bring dreams and associations, but these do not reverberate in the analyst's mind. The experience is of dryness—a dearth of memory, that may at times leave the analyst with a sense of exclusion from the patient's internal world.

The first category of patients expresses a conviction of intrusion into the primal scene; the second indicates an inability to imagine it. Both, in different ways, negate the primal scene and their exclusion from it.

Both these types of patients communicate through words as well as actions. In spite of the differences between them, they share an experience of something "unrepresentable" in their internal world, and both occupy a space that may be seen as either beyond or before the traditional analytic space of representations. I have previously suggested that the pathway through which the analyst can understand both these types of patients is via the countertransference. Here I identify other regressive processes that take place in the analyst's mind that enable her to make sense of psychic processes that have not reached representation. In the first clinical example, the patient expresses herself with a plethora of dreams and associations; eventually, a somatic process takes place between patient and analyst. In the second clinical example an image comes to the analyst's mind that opens up a link between the work of the analysis in the here and now and the patient's unrepresented experiences in infancy. In recent years several colleagues have emphasized the crucial relevance of the analyst's internal state of receptivity in the processing of patients' material that has not been fully elaborated (Birksted-Breen, 2009, 2012; Botella & Botella, 2005, 2013; Ferro, 2002; Ogden, 1997a, 1997b; Perelberg, 2009a, 2013). This chapter belongs to this tradition; it emphasizes the place of temporality in creating a triadic space in an analysis as it relates the here and now with the there and then in the work of *après-coup* (Perelberg, 2003, 2009a, 2013, 2016c). The chapter also traces the roots of this modern approach that relates the analyst's work of regression, time, and the creation of a triadic space to Freud's metapsychology.

The notion of "excess" and "closure" in the analytic process explored in this chapter are exemplified in two detailed clinical examples of analyses.

Clinical vignette: "Christina"

After the first summer break, Christina came to her session, lay on the couch in a state of intense anxiety, and said:

PATIENT (CHRISTINA): I came here excited today because I had three very intense dreams. I felt so excited. I still do.

At the beginning it was not sexual at all. *I met a friend. She said that we had not seen each other for a while, and I was very happy to see her too. I noticed that she had big breasts. Suddenly she transformed into a man, and we had sex. It was one of the most intense dreams I have ever had. I had orgasms, one after the other. He had them too. I lost count, but later I asked him how many orgasms he had. He said that it was five times. … I might be pregnant from all these orgasms. Because of the intensity, we did not use condoms. I might get pregnant from all this. How could I cover it up?* That was the dream. It was this experience of continuous satisfaction.

Then I had a second dream, still on Monday night. It was about *a tsunami that came over, and covered both Peter and me, this huge wave that was flooding everything. We were looking for our bags. We were on the beach, and there were some friends of ours with us. Peter took my hand, and I went with him into the sea, and it turned into a water park. It was then nice.* I now feel that my three dreams are like a flood.

ANALYST: You are feeling flooded and anxious about flooding me and yourself with your dreams. [My interpretation referred more to her state of excitation than to the content of the dreams themselves.]

P: Yes. [She cries.] They were so intense; especially the sexual one. I was also thinking that there would be barely time to tell you the three dreams, and then it would be time to go.

A: The experience of the dreams spills over into external reality.

P: Yes, especially the emotionality. Last night the dream was about *my Dad*. In the dream he *had run away and disappeared from my house. We thought he would kill himself, or commit suicide. In the whole dream we were looking for him, the three of us, my older sister, my Mum, and me. In the dream, my Mum phoned me and said, "I lost him."* In the dream *we found him.* I am supposed to now associate to the dream, but there is so much.

A: Coming back here after the break feels so overwhelming, so exciting, that it is like a tsunami that threatens you and Peter; it is the experience of meeting this woman you have not seen for a while, and now feel so happy to see; it is like having overwhelming, endless sex.

[Silence. Her state of agitation on the couch has subsided.]

P: Is it time?

[She is much calmer. There is a silence for about 3 minutes.]

P: In the end I managed to tell you about the three dreams and more. It's been ok.

Christina sounded calmer. There was another 5 minutes' silence. It was time.

In this session, Christina was able to express through her dreams the experience of excess, the too-muchness that marks her relationship to herself, her body. and to others. Coming back to see the analyst after the break was like a tsunami, or like having overwhelming sex. Yet I am also aware that this is a response to being excluded from the analyst's consulting room during the holiday break. It feels like a pressure to intrude and participate in a primal scene from which she is excluded.

In the second dream there is a wish for a man that will make the maternal waters less dangerous and will transform the waters of the sea into a water park.

In the third dream there is a search for a father that had been lost by the mother ("I lost him"), a search for the paternal function that will institute the boundaries and containment that Christina also hopes the analysis will bring her.

In the following session she said how much relief she had experienced in the previous session, being able to tell me all the dreams and feeling that I had understood her.

Christina is an attractive, successful American architect. She is the middle one of three sisters. Her husband is a medical doctor, and the couple themselves have three daughters. One is reminded that the material to which one has access in an analysis is that which has escaped from the maturation process and is a source of anxiety and suffering for the patient.

The eroticization of an experience of vulnerability is present from the outset of this analysis. Later we were to explore her experience of confusion as a very young child and her experience of being overexposed to her parents' sexuality—a reminder of Ferenczi's work on the confusion of tongues between adults and children (1932). This is also what Laplanche (1987, 1999) has referred to as "the fundamental anthropological situation" that relates to the infant's unpreparedness for the sexually saturated world of the adults.

A few years later

It is now some years later in Christina's analysis. The experience of excess, of elements that cannot be contained within the domain of the representable, is still present, but she can now become aware of such experiences as they express themselves in a session. The fusion of sexuality and aggression has now come to the fore.

On Monday, Christina brought a nightmare:

P: *The planets had somehow got together, they had ceased to be each in their own orbit. They came together in a massive explosion, and the world finished in a catastrophe.*

She was coughing throughout the session and told me this dream while coughing. [I had a sense that all her viruses were exploding into the room, and that I was catching her cold. I wondered what was going on.] While coughing, Christina talked about how she was not contagious, she had checked with the doctor. In the same breath she told me that both her husband and her two younger children had caught that cough.

I said to her that she wished that we would be merged together, like the planets, in this massive explosion of coughing. She continued to cough.

On Tuesday she said that she had not wanted to come. She wanted to write to me and say that she wasn't coming. She did not wish to contaminate me with her virus. She also had a sick feeling in her stomach. For quite a while she talked about feeling sick, while coughing. She felt disgusting with her virus. She felt that I would be thinking that I did not wish her to be there, that she was disgusting, and she made me sick. As she talked about it, her words felt like actions; they had an impact on me, and I started to feel sick in the way she was describing. I had a sense of violence and something also eroticized taking place.

Christina was reminded of a horror movie she had seen, where two toy animals had eaten each other up, with blood splashing everywhere. It had been a most horrific scene that had left her feeling sickened. All this had taken place in a child's bedroom. Then, on the following morning, the child in the film, Eleanor, had spoken in a fake voice, a fake way of relating to her toys, as if she were a parent speaking to a child, pretending everything was nice.

I said that she was describing the experience of the previous session and also today, this explosive scene: her coughing and the viruses that she felt that she was bringing into the room were equivalent to this horrific scene of the animals devouring each other. She felt that she was like the girl, pretending everything was all right, in a fake way, while this nightmare was going on in the session. As I was speaking, her cough totally stopped. There was a sense of calm in the room.

A dream that is recounted at the beginning of the first session of the week anticipates an experience that will become alive in the consulting room: in Christina's words, "the planets had somehow got together, they had ceased to be each in their own orbit. They came together in a massive explosion and the world finished in a catastrophe." The dream itself, although it contains an "endopsychic perception" of an experience of excess, is not in itself enough to contain the experience that is concretely projected through the coughing, and this has a physical impact on the analyst.[2] "The planets cease to be each in their orbit": I understood this retrospectively as a process of excorporation.[3] The associations at the second session described present a scene of violence and orality, through the animals mutually devouring each other. The experience of excess, of flooding—of, indeed, being devoured—was again very much present, as the account provoked a physical reaction in me. I was also surprised that we managed to elaborate and process it in the context of one session.

One can see the way in which both analyst and patient felt much calmer at the end of the Tuesday session. A process of —for the most part unconscious—psychic elaboration took place in these two sessions, via the analyst's elaboration of her own experience.

I now turn to another analysis, of a patient who made an impact on the analyst through his withholding. Nevertheless an important process of transformation takes place.

Clinical vignette: "Boris"

Boris's words flowed uninterruptedly throughout his sessions, with little resonance or affect. He brought dreams, associations, and interpretations himself. His speech had a machine-like quality. He induced in me a state that was slightly detached and also somewhat immobilized. I was, at the same time, aware of having, from the outset, thoughts about a traumatic experience that could not be fully put into words. Boris used to go to the toilet before and after each session, and this gave me a sense of something that was not being contained in the sessions themselves. His mode of communication had a mechanical quality. For instance, in the first few months he could spend part of the session describing his long journey from home to the consulting room and his need to get to the toilet in time—the long way from home to his analysis. Mostly he would describe streets, buildings, buses, and trains. Any description of meeting people in the early mornings as he came to his sessions contained some menacing quality—like, for instance, the fact that he would find himself walking behind a woman in the alleyway that went from his street to the train station. Would she be frightened of him, or was he of her? The links between these scenes and the experience of himself in the consulting room were spelt out but did not seem to reverberate with actual, live meaning.It was quite some time into his analysis, however, before Boris told me that after each session he would go to a nearby cafe to write notes about the session. These notes also contained his thoughts about the session; he would then search the psychoanalytic literature in order to look up references that felt relevant to his thoughts. He was his own analyst, and his analysis was conducted by himself, away from the consulting room. I was to be excluded from this whole process.

I had a dual experience of Boris: on the one hand, the flooding with words, the excess that had to be evacuated into the toilet or to be expressed before and after the session, and, on the other hand, the distance he kept, a sense of unreachability and closure in this process. Thoughts about danger, threat, and trauma were somewhat present in my mind, and I thought that these were the various ways in which he tried to find containment for himself and to feel safe.

Boris was born in Italy and was working in London as an economist. He was married and had three children. Talking of his early life, Boris told me that his mother had been seriously ill, of some unspecific illness, when he was born. He said that his father had taken him home from hospital and had looked after him. He thought that it had taken two weeks for his mother to come back. There was thus a reference to an early traumatic beginning, marked by his mother's absence and the threat to her life that his birth had inflicted on her.

A couple of years into analysis Boris had a dream that *he was surrounded by glass and could not reach the people around him.* This perfectly captured my experience of being with him in the room. As he related the dream, I had a visual image, which I communicated to him: this makes me think of a baby in an incubator. [The image I had in mind had been very precise; it referred to a blue glass incubator.]

Boris was very struck by this. At the following session he said that he had spoken to his mother and found out that actually his father had not taken him home with him when his mother was ill in hospital. He had stayed in hospital with her for the three weeks, but she was so ill that she had not been able to pick him up. He had himself spent some time in an incubator.

This was a striking new piece of information that brought a different narrative to the beginnings of Boris's life. It was something that he had not known about and obviously could not have any recollection of. It gave an uncanny new meaning to my experience of him in the analysis. A past that had not been registered at the representational level at the time that it had occurred had been repeated in the relationship to me in the analysis: the whole experience of having to provide containment for himself, as there was no mother available to carry him in her arms or to attend to his needs. The narrative of the dream, together with my own experience of him in the consulting room, had led to a visual image that I then put into words, which led to some new information about his life. We were in the domain of the unthought known (Bollas, 1987).

A few weeks before the session, a traumatic and shocking event had taken place at Boris's youngest son's school. A 5-year-old boy had been sexually assaulted by three 8-year-old children, who had put soap inside his anus. Boris's youngest son, who was also 5 years old at the time, had run to call a teacher, who came to the toilet and stopped what was going on. His son had since been bullied by the other children. Two days had passed before Boris spoke about it in the session, and he could then take the decision to go to the school himself and speak to the teachers about what had taken place. His initial reaction had been one of utter passivity and detachment. The transferential aspect of him experiencing himself as the 5-year-old who was being sodomized in the sessions by my simply speaking to him did not escape us, and I interpreted this to him. This prompted him to go to the school, and eventually he and his wife decided to take their child out of this school. Boris was, however, extremely upset about his lack of immediate action and passivity, although he also turned this into masochistic self-blaming. This event also evoked for him episodes of being bullied at school as a child himself and feeling unable to let people know.

The following is a session a few weeks later, the first session after a half-term break of a week. Boris missed the Monday session, as he was away; he came back on Tuesday.

PATIENT (BORIS): I had a dream last night. In the first part *I was going to leak some documents to* The Guardian. *They contained embarrassing information, and they were going to force the resignation of the Chancellor of the Exchequer. I was running through some suburban streets that looked like the roads where my parents live, somewhat more prosperous—which make me think more about this area where you live. I was being chased by a black car, the police. I had the feeling that I was not going to get the document out to the journalist. It was something to do with my son's school, about child abuse. I knew I was going to be arrested, so I started shouting it out loud in the street so that the information would be imparted …*

Then I was arrested and handcuffed with my hands behind my back; the cuffs were brown and red, and this meant that I was going to serve a life-sentence. I was protesting that I could not be condemned without a trial, but my protests were falling on deaf ears. I was taken to a mental hospital. There was a journalist around, who was sympathetic to what was happening to me but was unable to stop anything. I was secured on a chair; a woman, who was a long-term resident, half crazy, and a kind of matron, arrived. This unpleasant character was inflicting a punishment on me. She shaved my hair with a razor. It reminds me of pubic hair being shaved before some operation. She started at the top of my head and was very rough, uncaring. While she was doing this, there was a screen, so that I was separated from the others by glass. The journalist was there but could not stop what was going on. But he could ensure that this glass door was somewhat ajar, not completely closed, so I was not isolated with her.

[He pauses.]

[I am thinking that Boris sounds detached from the dream, but not as detached as he usually is. The glass door is perhaps a bit ajar. … I had also paid attention to the word "leak".]

P: I can only presume that this dream was about a deeper fear of returning to the analysis here. Although you had suggested before my sense of fear, I don't have access to these feelings …

I was struck by the image of the glass cubicle. It resonates with the last session before the break, your thoughts about my experience of being separated at birth by glass from my mother. I had always thought that my father had taken me home when my mother was ill and had to stay in hospital, but she told me now that I was in hospital with her for the three weeks after I was born. She had to stay in hospital as she was so ill, and I stayed with her. She could not pick me up, and I had to spend a lot of time in an incubator. She was on her guard about me asking her about it. Why did I want to know?

… I thought on my way here that perhaps it was hopeful that my feelings about you were distributed between the journalist, the matron, and the police officer … I woke up when I was being shaved … It was not as if the emotion was absent, but it was muted, low level … I am thinking about the glass cubicle and the door being left ajar … I was being handcuffed with brown and red handcuffs that meant a life sentence, 25 years. The colours were somehow organic, brown and red.

A: Blood and faeces …

[I had in mind all the sessions with the material about toilets and soiling himself as a child, the consequences for him now, a life sentence.]

P: Yes! I had this same thought on my way here. It was something about the helplessness of the situation in which I found myself on that chair. It could have been the couch. I also think that it relates to everything that happened with Tony [his youngest son].

[I had the thought that the one helpless on the chair is also me, the way I can feel handcuffed with very little movement. I noted that he responded to my interpretations by saying he had thought about that himself.]

A: … you feel helpless and have to do it all by yourself. You want to pass on the information that child abuse has taken place … but the tyrannical Chancellor of the Exchequer in yourself as well as myself does not want to know …

[He seems thoughtful.]

"I did feel more in touch in this session", he says. It is time.

Discussion

There is something of a paradox in Boris's analysis in the way in which words and thoughts can be denuded of meaning and depth because of the lack of accompanying affect, of libidinal investment. As he describes the dream, he is aware of various potential layers of meaning contained in the manifest content of the dream. However, he conveys his states of mind through interplay between "leaking" and withholding—the excess that floods outside the consulting room through his actions on the one hand, and the flowing of words without libidinal investment in the consulting room on the other. To fully know what he lets me know is to take away the powers of a tyrannical part of him. He comes to his sessions to his guardian/analyst, but he also runs away from the sessions as a fugitive from the police. He wishes to tell someone that sexual abuse is taking place, but he is confused as to who is abusing whom.

Boris's masochism registers my interpretations as abusive and as sodomizing him. I am experienced as half-crazy, unpleasant, and punitive. I am also a castrator, in the way I shave his hair and leave him feeling exposed. He is, at the same time, unaware of the way he leaves me paralysed, on the other side of the glass. The journalist can do nothing but watch or report. What strikes me the most about the session is not the content of his narrative, but the impact that he has on me. It is through my own experience of feeling handcuffed by his blood and faeces, his excesses, that the meaning of a traumatic event that involves abuse and persecution is reached. This session feels like a transformation of the scene of sexual abuse between the children in the toilet. Boris had initially felt totally paralysed in relation to that scene; the work we did together on that session enabled him to take an active role as a father.

In this session, the dream also has links with the glass incubator that I had visualized a few weeks earlier, the experience of total abandonment, helplessness, and confusion. The image that was formed in my mind and then put into words enabled a process of transformation and movement to take place.

> … images originate from perceptions and are repetitions of them. So that originally the mere existence of the image serves as a guarantee of the reality of what is imagined. The contrast between what is subjective and what is objective does not exist from the first. It only arises from the faculty which thought possesses for reviving a thing that has once been perceived, by reproducing it as an image, without its being necessary for the external object still to be present. Thus the first and immediate aim of the process of testing reality is not to discover an object in real perception corresponding to what is imagined, but to rediscover such an object …".
>
> (Freud, 1925h, p. 220)

"A thing that has once been perceived" is reproduced as an image. In this specific clinical example, a perceptual experience of the patient, never before put into words, is unconsciously conveyed to the analyst, who is then able to produce an image.

Different time dimensions are present. The experience I have of being with him over the years of his analysis reach representation in his dream of being surrounded by glass. This dream, which achieved figurability in my mind through an image and was transformed through my interpretation, led to the reappropriation of an infantile experience at birth: the scene between the 5-year-old children in the lavatory indicates the eroticization, *après-coup*, of the earlier experience of helplessness. Now all this gains further representation in the narrative of the dream in this session, which also elaborates and anticipates that which takes place in the session itself.[4]

The session has a different feel from a few years earlier. Boris himself refers to "muted" feelings or a glass door that is half open. He is no longer completely alone with a half-crazy woman, a depressed mother, in the hospital, as there is a man, an observer part of himself, who can register and witness his traumatic experiences.

Drives and representations

Both these patients evoke fundamental questions about the amount of excitation that can be tolerated by each individual ego and the unconscious strategies developed to deal with overwhelming experiences in order to gain a sense of safety and protection. We are in the domain of what lies at the limit of representation and has to be communicated in other ways. Christina conveys constantly and more obviously an experience of an excess that cannot be tamed. The excess of representations themselves, expressed both in the number of dreams at each session and in the imagery provided, are paradoxically an indicator of an excess of excitation that has not been fully represented. Through his withdrawal in his sessions, Boris displays acting-out behaviour outside the sessions in an attempt to find his own solutions for something that would otherwise feel unmanageable and overwhelming.

Freud's work addressed this issue from the outset, in his concern with the relationship between the economic and the ideational factors in the mind, which, according to him, follow different vicissitudes. The notion of investment is at the core of Freud's understanding of psychic functioning. In a passage added in 1915 to the *Three Essays on the Theory of Sexuality* (1905d), Freud gives a definition of an instinct (drive, *Trieb*):

> By an "instinct" is provisionally to be understood the psychical representative of an endosomatic, continuously flowing source of stimulation, as contrasted with a "stimulus", which is set up by single excitations coming from without. The concept of instinct is thus one of those lying on the frontier between the mental and the physical.
>
> (1905d, p. 168)

It refers to something that has, by definition, not yet reached representation.

In the *Three Essays* (1905d), Freud also indicates that the first experiences of pleasure are derived from bodily needs necessary to the preservation of life, such as the oral activities of babies that are linked to feeding. It is only at a second stage that the sexual functions find relative autonomy in relation to the self-preservative instincts (Chemouni, 2013, p. 170). The corporal experiences are at the very origin of the constitution of the psyche, and it is only progressively and incompletely that they become constituted as psychic reality.

In *The Interpretation of Dreams* (1900a), Freud indicates that the psychic apparatus attempts to regulate its internal excitation. Unpleasure is linked to the accumulation of tension, whereas pleasure is linked to its discharge. This formulation gains complexity in the metapsychological papers, where Freud provides a model for the understanding of psychopathologies such as hysteria, obsessional neurosis, and phobias in terms of the different vicissitudes of the drives and representations.[5] Freud is concerned with the question of how the ego regulates the drives.

The notions of binding and unbinding are crucial here. They refer to the process whereby affect and representation become bound to each other as one moves from the Unconscious system to the Preconscious–Conscious. In the Unconscious, energy is unbound and mobile and the rules of primary process, such as displacement and condensation, dominate. The pleasure principle reigns, and there is an absence of thinking and a predominance of visual and sense impressions. Words are used as objects, and there is no sense of time. In the Preconscious–Conscious system, energy becomes bound, leading to the creation of a temporal sequence and a delay of motor discharge through secondary-process thinking.

In "Formulations on the Two Principles of Mental Functioning" (1911b), Freud indicates that in the primary system, which operates in the young infant in dreams and to a large extent in waking phantasies, the pleasure principle dominates the scene. With the introduction of the reality principle, phantasy life is split off and is kept free from reality testing (p. 222). The sexual impulses, however, remain under the dominance of the pleasure principle for longer. "This is the weak spot in our psychical organisation", Freud suggests (p. 223).

Narcissism: libidinal investment of the ego

With his paper "On Narcissism" (1914c), Freud emphasizes the discovery of the libidinal investment of the ego. This idea, in fact, antedates this paper. In 1892, when discussing hysteria, Freud already discussed the excessive amount of excitation in the ego that seeks discharge:

> Hysteria begins with the overwhelming of the ego, which is what paranoia leads to. The raising of tension at the primary experience of unpleasure is so great that the ego does not resist it and forms no psychical symptom but is obliged to allow a manifestation of discharge—usually an excessive expression of excitation. This first stage of hysteria may be described as "fright hysteria"; its primary symptom is the manifestation of fright accompanied by a gap in the psyche. It is still unknown up to how late an age this first hysterical overwhelming of the ego can occur.
>
> (Freud, Draft K, 1950 [1892–1899], p. 228)

The "gap in the psyche" is what escapes representation. In 1893, Freud indicated the different vicissitudes followed by "excessive amounts of excitation" and the corresponding ideas that are then forced out of the ego consciousness:

> The hysterical method of defence—for which, as we have seen, the possession of a particular proclivity is necessary—lies in the conversion of the excitation into a somatic innervation; and the advantage of this is that the incompatible idea is forced out of the ego's consciousness. In exchange, that consciousness now contains the physical reminiscence which has arisen through conversion (in our case, the patient's subjective sensations of smell) and suffers from the affect which is more or less clearly attached to precisely that reminiscence.
>
> (Freud, 1895d, p. 122)

Deleuze has described the "insistence of sensation in hysteria: 'the identity of an already-there and of an always-late, in excessive presence. Everywhere a presence acts directly on the nervous system, and makes impossible the putting-in-place or putting-at-a distance of a representation'" (in Shaviro, 1990, p. 29).

Freud identified a narcissistic component in the omnipotence of thought. It is not expressed cognitively, but it is the quality of the emotions present that determine its relationship with reality. This form of thinking is the inheritor of the infantile megalomania and expresses the omnipotence of desire (Chemouni, 2013, p. 33). In *Totem and Taboo*, Freud makes a link between this omnipotence of thought and sexualization, a kind of "libidinal hypercathexis of thinking" (1912–13, p. 89).

It is this process of eroticization of thought that one can identify in Christina's over-excitation: it was this that had profoundly interfered with her capacity to study and to work at the outset in her analysis, as expressed in the initial dreams recounted at the beginning of this chapter. It is also what interferes with Boris's capacity to engage with his own thoughts. He needs to protect himself from over-excitation by delibidinizing and decathecting his own thinking processes. Thinking without affect, however, becomes sterile and immobilized. This lack of binding between affect and representation interferes with his preconscious capacities and his capacity to relate to his objects, both internal and external.

Excess, trauma, and helplessness

In *Beyond the Pleasure Principle* (1920g) the binding of affect and representation becomes a characteristic of the life drives themselves, in contrast to the death drives. In the text, Freud suggests that this traumatic experience is at the origins of repression. In *Inhibitions, Symptoms and Anxiety* (1926d), Freud introduces a new element as he establishes a link between an excessive amount of excitation and the infant's experience of helplessness and trauma. Strachey writes in his introduction:

> The fundamental determinant of automatic anxiety is the occurrence of a traumatic situation; and the essence of this is an experience of helplessness on the part of the ego in the face of an accumulation of excitation, whether of external or of internal origin, which cannot be dealt with (p. 166). Anxiety "as a signal" is the response of the ego to the threat of the occurrence of a traumatic situation. Such a threat constitutes a situation of danger. Internal dangers change with the period of life (pp. 146–147), but they have a common characteristic, namely that they involve separation from, or loss of, a loved object, or a loss of its love (p. 151)—a loss or separation which might in various ways lead to an accumulation of unsatisfied

> desires and so to a situation of helplessness. Though Freud had not brought all these factors together before, each of them has a long previous history.
>
> (Strachey, 1926, p. 81)

This text brings forward the notion of trauma, the experience of helplessness of the newborn and its lack of capacity to regulate excitation. The presence of the object becomes crucial for a process of processing and containment to take place.

Freud goes back to the notion of the protective shield that he had already discussed in his "Project" (1950 [1895]):

> It is highly probable that the immediate precipitating causes of primal repressions are quantitative factors such as an excessive force of excitation and the breaking through of the protective shield against stimuli.
>
> (Freud, 1926d, p. 94)

> It is still an undeniable fact that in sexual abstinence, in improper interference with the course of sexual excitation or if the latter is diverted from being worked over psychically, anxiety arises directly out of libido; in other words, that the ego is reduced to a state of helplessness in the face of an excessive tension due to need, as it was in the situation of birth, and that anxiety is then generated.
>
> (1926d, p. 141)

In 1920, Freud discovered a drive that does not correspond to any representation but expresses itself in the repetition compulsion. This formulation is at the basis of Green's formulations on the negative (1998, 1999, 2001; see also Perelberg, 2005, Perelberg and Kohon, 2017), of the blank spaces without representation, of mental structures where representations have disappeared from theoretical descriptions. The substitution of the unconscious by the id constitutes a crucial shift in Freud's model in that the id is made of impulses, with no representations. When dealing with borderlines, one thinks about the compulsion to repeat, a clinical manifestation of the death drive. If dreams provide a paradigm for the topographical model of the mind, enactments in the analytic process are the paradigm for the structural model, governed by the compulsion to repeat that which has not reached representation. There are implications for a theory of technique: the role of the analyst is not that of interpreting what "is already there" in the mind of the patient but, rather, that of inaugurating the symbolic domain and the world of representations (see Perelberg, 1997c, p. 73). There is an emphasis on the quantitative factor, which is not reducible to the domain of phantasies.

This way of understanding phenomena is based on the premise of the disjunction between drives and representations. As a model, it differs from Klein's, since Susan Isaacs proposes that unconscious phantasies are "the primary content of unconscious mental processes" and "the mental corollary, the psychic representative of instinct" (1948, p. 81). The psychic space, as conceived by Klein, is filled with representation; drives and objects are intrinsically linked: "Phantasy is (in the first instance) the mental corollary, the psychic representative, of instinct. There is no impulse, no instinctual urge or response which is not experienced as unconscious phantasy" (Isaacs, 1948, p. 80). For Freud, there is always something that escapes full representation and is discharged, either outside or inside, through symptoms. The links between the mind and the body are there from the beginning, but one is not totally subsumed by the other. A crucial question becomes what happens to the ego when it is impotent or flooded in its attempts to face phantasy life.

For Klein, drives and objects are intrinsically linked.[6] In Bion's formulations, in contrast, beta-elements stand for that which is unthinkable, belong to the sensorial domain, and, in the terms of this chapter, have not (yet) reached representation. The transformation of beta-elements to alpha-elements requires the existence of an object that is capable of reverie. "Beta-elements stand for that which is unthinkable, being the domain of thoughts that have no thinker" (Bion, 1992, p. 313; see also 1962b). The process of having thoughts with a thinker implies the transformation of beta-elements into alpha-elements.

Bion suggests that this becomes possible in the relationship between infant and mother when normal projective identification is enabled and precludes the development of an alpha-function and therefore a differentiation of elements into conscious and unconscious.

For Klein, there is an intrinsic link between the bad (frustrating) object and persecutory anxiety (e.g., 1946, p. 101; 1948, p. 117;

1958, p. 81; 1975, p. 7). For Bion, the lack of transformation of beta-elements into alpha-elements does not mean that a bad object is there instead. The individual struggles with "nameless dread". He states:

> Normal development follows if the relationship between infant and breast permits the infant to project a feeling, say, that it is dying into the mother and to reintroject it after its sojourn in the breast has made it tolerable to the infant psyche. If the projection is not accepted by the mother the infant feels that its feeling that it is dying is stripped of such meaning as it has. It therefore reintrojects, not a fear of dying made tolerable, but a nameless dread.
>
> (Bion, 1962b, p. 116)

Levine, Reed, and Scarfone (2013) have pointed out a link between Freud's notion of the drive and Bion's (1962b) concept of beta-elements as proto-psychic forms not suitable to be thought about. Similarly to Freud's notion of the drive, beta-elements, according to these authors, "made an implicit demand ('turbulence') upon the psyche for work (alpha function)" (Levine, Reed, & Scarfone, 2013, p. 5). They refer to Green's (1975, 2005a) notion of "a tear in the fabric of the psyche", a failure in the capacity to represent. Scarfone also draws a parallel between Freud's "quota of affect" and Bion's beta elements (Scarfone, 2013, p. 89). Sebastian Kohon (2014) has suggested similarities between the concept of "drive" and Bion's beta-element, thus emphasizing the "economic" aspect present in Bion's formulations.

The line of argument in this chapter can be understood as closer to Bion's: non-neurotic individuals struggle with the overwhelming experience of no meaning—that is, the major opposition in Green's psychoanalytic universe is no longer that between manifest and latent content, but between meaning and no meaning (Reed, 2002, p. 344). As Reed and Baudry suggest:

> What is there instead of an object representation is a hole in the psyche, a nothing rather than no-thing. … This is not the province of symbolization but of absence, the realm of the "Dead Mother" to cite the title of Green's famous paper (1986b).
>
> (Reed & Baudry, 2005, p. 132)

The somatic representative of the drive is severed from the object representation.

The Botellas have indicated that with Freud's paper on constructions (1937d), "the role of the past takes a more complex turn" (Botella & Botella, 2013, p. 97):

> Quite often we do not succeed in bringing the patient to recollect what has been repressed. Instead of that, if the analysis is carried out correctly, we produce in him assured conviction of the truth of the reconstruction which achieves the same therapeutic result as the recaptured memory.
>
> (Freud, 1937d, pp. 265–266)

These ideas represent a shift not only in the theoretical premises of psychoanalysis, but in the theory of technique. They suggest the concept of figurability in order to account for the analyst's work in such cases. The analyst's work of figurability is not equivalent to reverie, as it contains the capacity to create a "substitutive scene" that is triggered by the negative of the patient's experience that is "inaccessible and without memory" and "equivalent to an earlier scene that cannot be reached". "It has the capacity of replacing the memory without recollection by a substitutive memory that is destined to become a screen memory" (Botella & Botella, 2013, p. 119). It becomes a pictographic representation in the absence of representation that refers to a "gap in the psyche" (Freud, Draft K, 1950 [1892–1899], p. 228; see also page 12 above). One is referring here not to the recovery of an object that had been destroyed, but to the construction of a representation that is happening in the here and now for the first time. An object needs to exist before it is destroyed.

This reassessment of the role of the past raises interesting questions, as the example of Boris indicated. The baby in the incubator emerged because of the analyst's association and vision, derived from an experience in the room. It was very striking to find out that there was a historical reality, until then unknown, that was being expressed in Boris's way of relating to the analyst. It is somewhat difficult to convey the impact that such an experience has for both patient and analyst that supports one's belief in the process.

Green has identified the element of splitting in the population that currently seeks an analysis. He considers that all other defences are secondary to it.

> The effects of splitting are numerous. They go from a protection of a secret zone of non-contact where the patient is completely alone (Balint, 1968; Fairbairn, 1940) and where his real self is protected (Winnicott, 1960, 1963) or again which hides part of his bisexuality (Winnicott, 1971b), to attacks on linking in his thought processes (Bion, 1957, 1959, 1970; Donnet & Green, 1973) and the projection of the bad part of the self and of the object (Klein, 1946) with a marked denial of reality.
>
> (Green, 1975, pp. 6–7)

When these mechanisms are used, the analyst is in touch with psychic reality, but either he feels cut off from an inaccessible part of it or he sees his interventions crumble, being perceived as a persecutor and intruder (Levine, Reed, & Scarfone, 2013, p. 13; see also Rosenfeld, 1971, 1987).

Boris belongs to this category of patient: patients who create an empty space in the analyst's mind (Perelberg, 2003; Pontalis, 1974). Indeed, he experienced the analyst as a persecutor and intruder. Boris fills the space with his words—filling it in order to empty it and avoid contact. In this process, Boris goes to a secret zone of no contact where the patient is completely alone (see above).

One is attempting to understand a population of patients who cannot be understood in terms of a psychic apparatus that is full of representations in the model of the first neurotics treated by Freud in the first two phases of his work (see also Kohon, 2007).

The internal foreign body

In *Studies on Hysteria* (1895d), Freud refers to the traumatic thus:

> We presume rather that the psychical trauma—or more precisely the memory of the trauma—*acts like a foreign body* which long after its entry must continue to be regarded as an agent that is still at work.
>
> (p. 6; italics added)

Freud is pointing out the way in which what is traumatic is un-absorbable by representation and inaccessible to symbolization. This will be Laplanche's point of departure for his theory of generalized seduction whereby "an adult proffers to a child verbal, non-verbal and even behavioural signifiers which are pregnant with unconscious sexual significations" (1987, p. 126). What makes the message into an enigma is connected with the dimensions that the messages are unconscious to the emitting adult themselves. The infant is a receptor of a sexual message that has not reached awareness in the consciousness of the adults. These enigmatic messages then become "unmetabolizable foreign bodies", incapable of being symbolized.

In different ways, both Boris and Christina present a sense of incomprehension facing the adult world. Boris's description of the glass that separates him from the world of others may be understood from this perspective as well.

It took quite a few years of analysis before Christina was able to tell me about a scene that she experienced as traumatic. She must have been 4 years old and had gone into her parents' room early in the morning with her younger sister: they were both in bed "under their covers" and suddenly sat up. Their father decided, at that moment, to explain to them how babies were made. She was left confused, but as she left her parents' room she had told her sister that they, too, were going to make a baby. Did she seduce her sister when she said this to her? One is literally listening to a narrative that is experienced as an excess that comes from the enigmatic parental message that the child cannot decipher. It is this infantile scene that was transformed into her first dream after the first holiday break, described at the beginning of this chapter. The excess depicted in the dream itself parallels the very experience of an unmetabolizable excess of excitation.

Descriptive and dynamic *après-coup*

Psychoanalytic work takes place in the *après-coup*: its force is derived from the link between the here-and-now, and there-and-then, the scene of the unconscious (Perelberg, 2009a). One of Freud's major discoveries in the analysis of Emma (1950 [1895]) and also of the Wolf Man (1918b) was that trauma is constructed twice, and neither is meaningful on its own (Laplanche & Pontalis, 1967). In the subsequent scenes of both these analyses, the invisible links with the infantile were delineated. Freud did not fully recognize in his conceptualization that these earlier scenes acquire the element of thirdness in the here-and-now of his interpretations. In addition to the scene of seduction witnessed by the Wolf Man aged 18 months and its transformation and elaboration into the dream of the wolves, aged 4, it is as a young adult, in the here-and-now of his analysis with Freud, that the two previous scenes acquired meaning. I am not emphasizing the chronological sequence so intensely sought by Freud in this analysis, but the crucial relevance of *the psychoanalytic model that he then inaugurates*. It is in the *après-coup* that a radical psychoanalytic understanding of time is initiated.

In previous works I have drawn a distinction between descriptive *après-coup* and dynamic *après-coup* (Perelberg, 2006, 2007, 2008b, 2009a).[7] Descriptive *après-coup* seems to have become present in colloquial psychoanalysis, and it simply means retrospective signification. Dynamic *après-coup*, on the other hand, includes different notions of temporality, such as fixation, regression, repetition compulsion, and the return of the repressed. These different notions of time refer to the heterochrony in psychoanalysis (Green, 2002b). Furthermore, the dynamic *après-coup* is inserted into a network of concepts such as trauma, castration, and infantile sexuality, giving a specific meaning to the whole body of Freud's theory (Perelberg, 2006). It is the linkage of *après-coup* to this network of concepts that gives it a metapsychological dimension. It is the temporality of the *après-coup*, establishing the links between the here and now and there and then, that marks the passage from a dyadic to a triadic structure in an analysis (Perelberg, 2013, p. 581). This chapter has traced the different moments in time when *après-coup* gave meaning to both Christina's and Boris's experiences.

Conclusion

I have revisited a contrast previously discussed between full and empty spaces in the analytic process.

The clinical examples refer to two patients whose suffering is presented in terms of "too much" or "too little" affective investment they have in themselves and their analysis. Christina expressed an excess of affects, somatization, and dreams that flooded her and her analyst. The examples of her sessions indicate how over-excited she felt at the beginning of her analysis, in her dreams of a tsunami and of an endless orgasm.

Boris expressed himself in this contrasting idiom of excess and closure, living in a space in which it was difficult for the analyst to intervene without being experienced as an intruder or a persecutor.

I have now come to think that what takes place cannot be accounted for with traditional concepts of countertransference and projective identification. Modern concepts such as excorporation and figurability are central to our understanding of the processes. The latter is exemplified in the session where the analyst had the vision of a baby in a blue incubator, an experience that gathered together a heterogeneity of material, derived from many sources. Previously unrepresented experiences gained representation through the analytic work. Through her own regressive movements—somatic, in one case, and hallucinatory in the other—the analyst is able to link current experiences in the analysis with the lost experiences of the infantile past.

Birksted-Breen has suggested that when working with patients who present a difficulty in their capacity to symbolize and represent, the analyst's reverie and use of metaphor or images

> acts as a third element that is felt to belong to some extent to both parties or to neither. … In operating as a third element, the pictorial image coming from the analyst's reverie fosters a greater psychic space and the necessary triangulation for the development of symbolisation.
>
> (2012, p. 831)

There is a close parallel between Birksted-Breen's ideas and mine. She is referring to the work of the psychoanalyst in a session and the relevance of reverie and taking time for a process of symbolization to be facilitated. I am in agreement with her; temporality itself is an essential element of thirdness in a psychoanalytic model. By definition psychoanalytic work takes place in the *après-coup* (Perelberg, 2009a). It is the link between the here-and-now and the there-and-then that inaugurates a psychoanalytic temporality and an opening to the future.

In both examples discussed in this chapter, the process of elaboration and working through takes place through a complex pathway of bringing together affect, representation, sensorial and somatic experiences, dreams, associations, and enactments as they are gathered and found meaning *après-coup* through analytic work.[8] A triadic structure is then inaugurated that links the here and now with the infantile experiences there and then (Perelberg, 2009a, 2013).

In our practice as analysts we know that it is always the next moment of a session, the next day, or the next year that might clarify something that has taken place earlier. In any given session, one may grasp the retrospective meaning of what has taken place and anticipate what will happen in future—the two aspects of *après-coup*. Something, nevertheless, is always being left out, the model being the navel of the dream, the contact with the unknown. There is a kind of reassurance in the process: by definition, one does not fully know the meaning of what is happening at any moment in time. In the words of Bataille, "I fail, no matter what I write, in this, that I should be linking the infinite—insane—richness of 'possible' to the precision of meaning" (1998, p. 38).

An analogy with music comes to mind. Elgar, in connection with his Enigma Variations, refers to the theme that is not played:

> The Enigma I will not explain—its "dark saying" must be left unguessed, and I warn you that the apparent connection between the variations and the theme is often of the slightest texture; further, through and over the whole set another and larger theme "goes", but it is not played.
>
> (Cadogan Hall Programme, 2014)

In the clinical examples in this chapter, the fragmentation of the experiences in the process of being gathered in the analysis are variations and transformations of original traumatic infantile experiences. It is the repetition of the trauma in the analytic process and its elaboration through the analytic listening that transforms a sequence of *coups* into *après-coup*, inaugurating a psychoanalytic temporality.

Notes

1 Britton has described two similar clinical situations that he designates as narcissistic detachment and narcissistic adherence (Britton, 2003, p. 174).

2 Freud first proposed the notion of "endopsychic perceptions" in a letter to Fliess dated 12 December 1897. He is referring to an inner

unconscious perception of one's mental functioning, originated internally and then projected outwards: "Can you imagine what 'endopsychic perceptions myths' are? The latest product of my mental labor. The dim inner perception of one's own psychic apparatus stimulates thought illusions, which of course are projected onto the outside and, characteristically, into the future and the beyond. Immortality, retribution, the entire beyond are all reflections of our psychic internal [world]. Meschugge? Psycho-mythology" (in Masson, 1985, p. 286). In "Delusions and Dreams in Jensen's Gradiva", Freud indicated the "perfect similarity" between the burial of Pompeii, depicted in Jensen's hero's dream and delusions, and the disappearance of his childhood past, combined with its preservation (1907a, p. 51).

3 For Freud, the first move of the primordial mind was to split between what is good and what is bad, what had to be taken in and what had to be thrown out. Freud here opposes introjection and ejection (not projection). Donnet and Green (1973) have contrasted incorporation with excorporation, distinguishing it from projection in order to characterize a mechanism that they identified in the psychotic individual. When psychic metabolization becomes impossible, the psyche attempts to get rid of extreme states of anxiety not only from the mind, but also the body. They suggest that different mechanisms exist in neurotic and psychotic patients. In the former, "representations which move from the unconscious through the preconscious to the conscious are then expressed through verbalisation" (Green, 1998, p. 654); for the latter, "the messages are directly evacuated from the unconscious and projected to the object outside, bypassing the working through that transforms them through the preconscious before their verbalisation" (p. 654).

4 These different moments in time act like a fractal. A fractal is a complex geometric structure in which each image contains a smaller copy of itself, the sequence appearing to recur infinitely. Each repetition reflects the larger structure. The importance of the notion of a fractal is its connection with Freud's notion of repetition compulsion and *après-coup* (Chervet, 2009; Perelberg, 2009a, 2013, p. 564).

5 In the first, the affect is discharged while the ideational content is repressed; in obsessional neurosis the ideational content is rejected, and the affect disappears via a reaction formation. In phobias the ideational content is displaced, and the quantitative element is transformed into anxiety (e.g. fear of the wolf instead of love for the father) (Freud, 1915e; see also 1905d, 1909d, 1918b).

6 Klein has, nevertheless, suggested the notion of memories in feelings; these are emotions and anxieties that go back to earliest infancy and

"often underline a cover memory". Klein offers this idea in her notes after the 64th session in her analysis of Richard. These "memories in feelings" are attached to unconscious phantasies that are explained in great detail: "This feeling was bound up with his memories of early childhood, revived by seeing their house again, and stirred up the love and concern for his father and the wish to renew the family life. As had been seen in connection with earlier material, the deserted and bombed house in "Z" also stood for his deserted mother. By reviving the past and experiencing love, Richard felt that he could undo or counteract his destructive desires and his identification with the Hitler-father." (Klein, 1961, p. 318)

7 At the Colloque de Deauville in 2005, before the publication of Laplanche's volume on *après-coup* (Problematique VI) in 2006.

8 Jean Claude Rolland (personal communication, 14 September 2014) suggested that an important aspect of my analytic work with Boris might be thought about in terms of *Nebenmensch*—a capacity to be in touch with a fellow human being, which Freud refers to in his "Project" (1950 [1895]). Although Freud does not explicitly refer to the mother–baby relationship, the notion of *Nebenmensch* refers to a quality of humanity that enables one to be profoundly in touch with the distressing experiences of the baby. The baby is then able to internalize the perceptual experiences of this fellow human being. Chris Mawson made a similar comment when checking this reference: "It is the recognition of humanity as a primary feature in the mother's orientating her 'perceptual apparatus' to her baby and that of the baby in orienting to the mother's response to his/her cries" (personal communication, 28 September 2014). Throughout his work Rolland has been particularly interested in how perceptual experiences may gain representation in the analytic process through language (2006, 2010, 2015). "Let us suppose that the object that furnishes the perception resembles the subject—a fellow human-being. If so, the theoretical interest [taken in it] is also explained by the fact that an object like this was simultaneously the [subject's] first satisfying object and further his first hostile object, as well as his sole helping power. For this reason it is in relation to a fellow human-being that a human-being learns to cognize. Then the *perceptual complexes* [italics added] proceeding from this fellow human-being will in part be new and non-comparable—his features, for instance, in the visual sphere; but other visual perceptions—e.g. those of the movements of his hands—will coincide in the subject with memories of quite similar visual impressions of his own, of his own body, [memories] which are associated with memories of movements experienced by himself." (Freud, 1950 [1895], p. 331)

3

NEGATIVE HALLUCINATIONS, DREAMS, AND HALLUCINATIONS

The framing structure and its representation in the analytic setting

The framing structure

Green states that when holding her infant, the mother leaves the impression of her arms on the child, and this constitutes a framing structure that contains, in her absence, the loss of the perception of the maternal object and a negative hallucination of it. The framing structure is the outcome of the internalization of the maternal environment created by maternal care. It is the "primordial matrix of the cathexis to come" (Green, 1986b, p. 166). The capacity for the negative hallucination of the mother lies at the origins of representation; it is against the background of negativity that future representations of the object are inscribed. This is the role of the negative in its structuring function (Green, 2005b, p. 161;[1] 2005c). From this perspective, negative hallucination precedes all theory of representation. The negative hallucination creates a potential space for the representation and investment of new objects and the conditions in which the activities of thinking and symbolization can take place.[2] In marking the role of the absent other in the constitution of the psyche, Green is following the traditions of both Winnicott and Bion. This is an absence as "an intermediary situation between presence … and loss" (Urribarri, 2005, p. 205). This leads to Green's statement that "the Psyche is the relationship between two bodies in which one is absent" (1995, pp. 69–76).[3]

The negative hallucination of the mother is a precondition for Freud's hallucinatory wish-fulfilment, for images, for phantasy life, and for thinking. It is also an indication of thirdness, as the mother's absence implicitly poses the question: "Where does she go when she goes away?" This is an implicit reference to the father. It is to him, as her lover, that she goes. The mother's absence and the activity of phantasy that her absence gives rise to within the framing structure lies at the heart of Green's formulation about the psychoanalytic setting itself.

What happens if these processes fail to take place and if a traumatic intrusion does not allow for absence that would enable a psychic space to be solidly constituted? What are the consequences for the beginnings of phantasy life if the mother is too terrifying for the child, like the psychotic mother, so that the child cannot internalize its framing structure? In his formulation of the "dead mother complex", Green (1986b) outlines the way in which maternal traumatism, the mother's depression and withdrawal from the child, has consequences for the constitution of the child's psyche, leaving psychic holes in the Unconscious, a loss of meaning—nothing, in Bion's terms (Bion, 1965, p. 79)—and an impairment of the capacity to represent and to separate the intra-psychic from the inter-subjective. There are implications for a theory of technique in that the role of the analyst is not that of interpreting what is already there in the mind of the patient; the analytic task becomes a process of constructing such meaning (Perelberg, 2003, 2015). Any manifestation of hatred in such an analysis is a consequence of this massive decathexis and secondary to it; if the analyst's interpretations are centred on the attacks on the setting, they will be futile and will not address the main problem (Green, 1986a).

Too much absence, Green suggests, leads to the sentiment of solitude, helplessness, and despair; a separation that lasts too long leads to the decathexis of the object (Winnicott, 1971b), as the patient's mind becomes filled with death, absence, or amnesia. An over-presence that is too frightening leads to a disorganizing, incomprehensible, claustrophobic internal and external world.

The following clinical vignette is an example of an analysis where one gained access to a terrifying maternal imago in the vicissitudes of the transference and countertransference.

Clinical vignette: "Carolina"

Carolina's analysis: tearing the fabric of the dream

One Wednesday morning Carolina came to her session and said:

PATIENT (CAROLINA): I can remember a dream that was horrendous. One of those dreams I tend to have and never remember.

Two words stand out: "against abortion". In the dream *I was struggling to tear the fabric of the dream.* It all felt reasonable in the dream. The words kept being repeated in my head throughout, as if it was chanting a (refrain). A knife was going to be pinned through my back. I was half asleep throughout and was telling myself that it was just a dream. *I was diving. There was also this cheese that had melted, and words were appearing written in cheese. Then I was diving in green murky waters. All the time my dream was like a piece of fabric, and I was trying to tear a way out of it. The waters were mud. I was mud. In the mud there were fish, seahorses, crabs—all these things in the mud that turned into glass, shards of glass. They were cutting me inside.*

It was a horrific dream. My half-awake state lasted for a long time until I could sleep again.

[She half laughed.]

[Very long silence.]

I commented that it was horrific, and yet she was half laughing: I wonder if the laughter became a way of disowning such a horrific dream.

She said that it was just a dream.

ANALYST: It is an experience that you went through for a long time during the night.

[Silence.]

P: I can't think seriously about it. … But it was scary to be in my room as I went through it …

[I was thinking about her coming in with her usual smiling face, in a rush …]

A: Perhaps there is a link between these dreams that don't feel real and your constant state of activity, trying to escape from this horrific dream life.

Carolina said that it reminded her of a dream that she had had a long time ago.

I was in a horror film, a pastiche of Scream. It was in a big house with a big garden, a perfect setting for a horror dream. Eventually the ambulance arrived. Someone had gone missing, and it was me. There was a crazy lunatic murderer out there. The ambulance finally came, they were carrying someone on a stretcher who had died, and it was me. There was a balloon-shaped membrane coming out of me, obscuring my face. I think that membrane was full of blood that was threatening to burst out. It was just like when I was trying to tear myself out of the dream.

[Silence.]

A: It is so horrific; in several ways you have to keep out of the dream. It is a film, and you are watching what is happening [addressing her relationship to the dream rather than the content].

P: I am frightened but I am also frightening. Like in today's dream the mud is me. It is an engulfing thing that prevents me from moving. It is more comfortable for me to think of myself as the scared creature. The "it" that scares me is the unknown factor of how mad I am. I associate this dream to a Lorca play that was made into a film: *Blood Wedding*. The mother in this film anticipated all the horror that was about to happen. She said: "There is a scream in my ear that is always rising up."

She anticipated all the blood that was to follow, and she could not do anything about it. The mother's scream is of anguish and foreboding: she anticipates it all and cannot stop it. My fear is that if I get in touch with it all, I will never get out of it, I will never be able to stop the anguish, the tears, and the overwhelming sadness. [She cries.]

She does not really scream, Carolina adds.

A: The horrific world that you connect with a mother's screams that intrudes into you, your heart; you fear you cannot do anything about it.

[Silence.]

P: I wonder why this dream happens now.

A: When thinking about the knife in your back, I wonder if it is fear of me too, and of what is on my mind [thinking of the very first consultation, when she had talked about "Fawlty Towers", in which a seemingly inoffensive Portuguese waiter was apparently capable of murder].

P: I wonder about the word "abortion" in the dream. I know that my mother wanted to abort me ...

[Silence.]

Analyst [having in mind the fact that I had cancelled two sessions this week]: I am thinking of this week, with just three sessions, that feel so disturbing. Like an abortion.

In this session there is a profound link between the nightmare of the previous night, a repetitive childhood dream, and the experience in the transference of a maternal imago that evokes death rather than life.

Background

Carolina was the youngest of four children, the other three being boys. The family was originally from a Latin American country. Carolina had moved to London a few years earlier because of her work, and the analysis took place in her native language. Carolina remembers feeling frightened and confused in the world as a child, not fully understanding what was going on around her and the nature of people's relationships to each other. From very early on she remembers feeling terrified of her mother, whose behaviour felt unpredictable. She herself felt monstrous and thought her mother hated her. She remembers being kept up until late at night watching horror movies with her mother, who would then pretend that she was herself a monster—Dracula, or a vampire—and then laugh in a most violent way. Carolina was not sure whether she was more frightened of the monster or of not knowing whether her mother was being serious or joking. Carolina felt that she would have preferred her mother to actually be a monster to the uncertainty of not knowing. She felt unable to separate reality from the nightmarish world of the horror films.

Carolina was told by her mother that she had wanted to abort her; her mother had also found her a difficult baby, who was always crying and dissatisfied. Her mother had taught her not to cry by closing the bedroom door and leaving her to cry until she stopped.

When Carolina was between the ages of 6 and 9, her mother developed an extensive narrative about witches. The world was populated by witches, good and bad. She was a good witch; the bad witches were always trying to snatch children, so one had to be careful. At night her mother went out on her broomstick. Sometimes Carolina went to the window to try to catch sight of her, and several times thought she had seen her flying by.

When the family moved to another city, Carolina's mother told her that their new home had been built in a cemetery. There was a graveyard opposite the house, and she thought that it was an evil street. Carolina was terrified at night as she lay awake, listening to deep clanking noises coming from a nearby market. Her mother said that they were killing animals; sometimes Carolina thought that they were killing people. The world felt terrifying and unpredictable.

Carolina did not have much contact with her two older brothers, quite a few years her senior, who had remained in their city of origin. Her younger brother, in contrast to herself, seemed to be a happy being. He was liked by everyone, and he ran around, carefree and contented. As she grew up, her father provided a sense of a minimal protection when he was at home. He worked long hours and used to come home very late. Carolina experienced him, nevertheless, as distant and demanding, and she felt that she was a disappointment to him. She remembers once going to his office on the top floor, where she was expected to do an old paper as practice for a school entrance exam. The problem was that it was about fractions, which she hadn't yet studied and didn't know anything about. So when her father told her to pick an answer from the multiple-choice test, she assumed that the big numbers would be the right answers. Her father was frustrated with her, saying: "No, no, no, pick another one." She had no idea what she was supposed to do. This interaction seemed to characterize some of her experience of being in the world, and later in the analysis she consistently felt she was being asked to solve fractions that she didn't understand. She tried to overcome this experience by frantically pretending to fit in.

Carolina was nevertheless very bright, and she worked hard at school; she did well and was accepted by a prestigious university in her country. When she finished, she embarked on a successful career of her choice. At the time she came for analysis, Carolina had come to London to work for a prestigious law firm.

The analysis

On the eve of starting her five-times-a-week analysis, Carolina phoned to say that her father had died. Her boss at work had given her a month off, so that she could travel home to be with her mother. The beginning of her analysis was thus marked by her father's death and by her absence in order to be with her mother. In many ways this configuration set the tone of the early months of her analysis, marked by the register of the repetition compulsion. The father had gone, and we were both going to be left to deal with her being with the mad mother.

During the first few months of our work together, Carolina was in a traumatized state as a result of her father's death. Progressively, I realized that there was a strong sense of absence, of lack of contact, of bewilderment as she spoke about feeling lost in the world. At the time she used to have terrifying nightmares, which she would have few recollections of, apart from waking up screaming in terror in the middle of the night. These nightmares without words allude to the negative hallucination of thought and to Carolina's inability to express herself in words that conveyed meaning. They belonged to the order of that which was, until then, unrepresented. In the sessions I was struck by her constant activity at work: she was always in "action mode". Her narrative in the sessions had an evacuatory quality. She could speak continuously for the 50 minutes of each session without giving me any space to make a comment. There was a force in her speech that some time later I referred to as a machine gun (as it evoked a sense of murder and war). In the countertransference I sometimes felt totally squashed, empty, and depleted at the end of such sessions.

What Carolina brought to her analysis was the experience of not possessing a thinking structure that allowed her to process experiences into thoughts. Once she had a dream in which *she had lost the top of her skull, and there were worms inside her head, spilling out.* Coming to analysis and exposing herself to the mind of another as well as her own was the most dangerous situation she could put herself into.

The nightmare I described at the beginning captures so many aspects of her experience of being at work and in analysis. Trying to tear the fabric of the dream represents her attempt to get rid of this experience of being trapped inside the mother's body, the mother's mind, her own mind, and that of the analyst. Her mother, who had wanted to abort her, is experienced as the source of death, terrors, and nightmares, rather than as life-giving. The waters of her womb are murky and contain fish, seahorses, crabs: primitive things, not a human foetus. They turn into glass—shards of glass that cut from the inside. The world of *Blood Wedding* is tragic: the men die in knife fights, and the women survive on their own. They are left with the mother's scream. The characters don't have names but are referred to in terms of their positions in the family: Mother, Father, Brother, Bride, Bridegroom. This is the world of Spanish South America, with the inherent violence of the Spanish conquest and later consecutive dictatorships. It is this tragic, excessive, nameless world that we attempted to navigate in the analysis (Perelberg, 2015).

In the present, too, Carolina was always left confused, after her interactions with her mother, as to whether something had or had not really happened. This was minimally present in the transference as well as the countertransference, although a few years were to go by before it became possible to experience this more directly. An association that occurred to me in that initial phase of work together was derived from the film *Gaslight*, in which the victim is gradually manipulated into doubting her own reality.[4] *Time Out* wrote about the 1940 version of the film: "Lurking menace hangs in the air like a fog, the atmosphere is electric, and Wynyard suffers exquisitely as she struggles to keep dementia at bay" (Wikipedia).

The hallucination of the knife

Three years into her analysis, Carolina had a hallucination of a knife that persecuted her throughout a whole weekend. She said that it was neither a dream nor a vision: this knife floated around her all the time. She could not get rid of it, and she continued to see it in her dreams as well as when she woke up. She felt terrified, claustrophobic, and very disturbed. In my countertransference I also felt alarmed and anxious that the psychotic part of her personality was becoming more prominent.

The meaning of the knife was overdetermined. Carolina had met a man and had been invited to spend the weekend at his mother's house. The knife was an attack on everything that was nascent at the time: This knife enabled her to cut herself off into a narcissistic enclosure, where everything else paled into insignificance and became meaningless. It felt like a fundamental "no" she was saying to herself and to me, a pure culture of the work of the negative: "I can say no to everything."

The knife, ever-present throughout the weekend, reminded me of *Blood Wedding*. The Mother says, at the beginning of Act I: "The knife, the knife … Damn all of them and the scoundrel who invented them … even the tiniest knife … and mattocks and pitchforks … Everything that can cut a man's body …" (Lorca, 1987, p. 3). There was something inexorably present and foreboding about it. One was left in a universe provided by the crazy Mother. Could analysis introduce a difference to the mother's predictions?

This episode is also reminiscent of the Wolf Man's negative hallucination of cutting his finger off.[5]

The hallucination of the knife took place over a weekend, away from the analysis. It was to be expected that we would eventually confront something in the consulting room itself.

The human-sized wasp

In a session a few weeks later, a wasp got into the room and was buzzing around the window, sometimes circling the room. I could sense Carolina's paralysis and terror but did not say anything. I thought that we were both being enveloped in a kind of claustrophobic, paralysing terror that could not be put into words. The atmosphere was extremely tense, and I waited in a silence that persisted until the end of the session. "Lurking menace hangs in the air like a fog, the atmosphere is electric. …"

At the following session Carolina told me that she had seen a woman-sized wasp hanging by the door throughout the session and had felt paralysed.

CAROLINA: The giant human-sized wasp was definitely by the door. There was a poised elegance about it as it was hanging there, I was thinking that I am carrying on talking here, you try to introduce another point of view, and I feel like I'm being attacked. You say it very gently, politely, and all I can hear is the attack. It is very real.

If there is a frequent image I associate with my mother, it

is that of a Rottweiler on a chain, barking and barking and the sharp teeth showing, trying to get rid of the chain in order to attack you and kill you. My mother would show me her Dracula teeth when I was older to scare me, but she told me that she did it even when I was a baby, and I would cry. … like the human-sized wasp I saw here. It was not like the Rottweiler straining at its lead. It is straining because it wants to kill you. The wasp is more meditative, biding its time. But it is also dangerous. It can eventually kill you.

A: What there is in common is the sense of danger and threat.

P: The wasp had not yet decided if it was going to kill you. It is not as violently terrifying. When there was a wasp in the room, I couldn't relax, as I couldn't predict what would happen. … Some sessions I can leave unscathed, but I never know. Outside I can keep an eye on them, but they are more elusive and harder to pin down. Here is the same, meaning that it is harder to pin down for me, it buzzes away. I think of them as dangerous.

A: This is your experience of being here: fear, danger. … Of me, but perhaps also of yourself.

P: The worst is to think of all this aggression in me …

Images, dreams, hallucinations: some reflections

In *The Interpretation of Dreams*, Freud postulated "conditions of representability" "as one of the characteristics of the dream work" (1900a, p. 499). Thoughts are expressed in images that condense a multitude of thoughts or people, giving rise to "composite images" (p. 324). Images are the oldest form of registering an experience: they are closer to the Unconscious. The word "image" is derived from "imago", the representation of the ancestor at the very moment of its disappearance—that is, at the moment of mourning (Rolland, 2015, p. 107). The presence of an image is linked to the absence of the object. This absence is at the origin of the hallucinatory wish-fulfilment of infancy whereby the baby tries to reproduce the experience of satisfaction.

> An essential component of this experience of satisfaction is a particular perception (that of nourishment, in our example),

> the mnemic image of which remains associated thenceforward with the memory trace of the excitation produced by the need. As a result of the link that has thus been established, next time this need arises a psychical impulse will at once emerge which will seek to re-cathect the mnemic image of the perception and to re-evoke the perception itself, that is to say, to re-establish the situation of the original satisfaction.
>
> (Freud, 1900a, pp. 565–566)

In "Negation", Freud postulates that images originated from perceptual experiences:

> … all presentations originate from perceptions and are repetitions of them. Thus originally the mere existence of a presentation was a guarantee of the reality of what was presented. The antithesis between subjective and objective does not exist from the first. It only comes into being from the fact that thinking possesses the capacity to bring before the mind once more something that has once been perceived, by reproducing it as a presentation without the external object having still to be there.
>
> (Freud, 1925h, p. 238)

Images are polysemic and irradiate in multiple directions, evoking different layers of experience. The analytic process brings forth, from time to time, images that are like the mythogram of the individual history in that they organize the affective experience of the individual (Rolland, 2015, p. 143).

In ordinary development one can trace a sequence from the experience of satisfaction, the absence of the object, the negative hallucination in its structuring function, to hallucinatory wish-fulfilment—all of which lie at the origin of representation.

Images are the material of the hallucination wish-fulfilment, of dreams, phantasies, and works of art, but they can also be the stuff of hallucinations, as in the case of Freud's hysterics, the most famous of whom might be Anna O, who was treated by Breuer (Freud, 1895d). She had hallucinations of snakes when she was looking after her father, who was ill and was about to die, leaving her at the mercy of a melancholic maternal imago (Perelberg, 1999a). These hallucinations represent a failure in the capacity for an internal, unconscious representation that are turned into perceptions. Freud considered that the aim of the treatment was to replace such images with narratives that would tell their stories.

Hallucinations can be understood as a first attempt at self-cure, as in the Schreber case (Freud, 1911c). The delusional formation "is in reality an attempt at recovery, a process of reconstruction" (p. 71). "This attempt at recovery, which observers mistake for the disease itself, does not, as in paranoia, make use of projection, but employs a hallucinatory (hysterical) mechanism" (p. 77).[6]

Bion understood hallucinations as the outcome of mental processes that destroy alpha-elements and reduce them to fragments that can be thought about but have to be evacuated. They are projected into the outside world, giving rise to bizarre objects. The component of self-cure is, however, also present in Bion's formulations. He believes that what is evacuated in hallucinations are sensory elements that still have some elements of meaning attached to them:

> The "peculiarity" of the dream to the psychotic is not its irrationality, incoherence and fragmentation, but its revelation of objects which are felt by the patient to be whole objects and therefore fit and proper reasons for the powerful feelings of guilt and depression.
>
> (Bion, 1958, p. 80)

Thus for Bion, too, images have a curative dimension.

My patient Carolina's hallucination of the knife indicated an aspect of her experience that had remained foreclosed in her life: a terror of a primitive, murderous maternal imago and her own identification with this mother.[7] The production of a hallucination meant, however, that something was also active in the present, in the immediacy of the transference. In the manner of dreams, there are at least two different sources at work: a mnemic trace inscribed in infancy linked to a traumatism and a current perception that has a capacity to be linked to the mnemic trace. It is therefore multiple representations that give rise to an image (see Birksted-Breen, 2012). In the subsequent hallucination of the wasp, the fear of unpredictability in both patient and analyst is projected onto the wasp that was buzzing in an arbitrary way around the room. Through her hallucination my patient had deposited that wasp in the corner of the room, by the door, where she could keep an eye on it. The possibility of danger was dramatized, but it was now under her omnipotent control. A significant transformation took place between the hallucination of the knife, which indicated a moment when she felt herself to be in mortal danger, and the hallucination of the wasp, a few weeks later, where the danger was experienced as being more under her control.

If negative hallucination is the common matrix between dreams and hallucinations, they cannot be superimposed on each other (Green, 1999, p. 276). It is my belief that, in contrast to a dream image, which is a product of condensation and displacement and an outcome of the dream work, when one is dealing with hallucinations, meaning has yet to be achieved. Freud believed that while images condense, hallucinations decompose through splitting (1911c, p. 48). Dream images are internal, the products of psychic reality; hallucinations are an expression of unprocessed material that has been expelled and is experienced as coming from external reality. Schreber's fear of the end of the world was the projection of an internal catastrophe (p. 70); his "rays of god" are a projection of his libidinal cathexes (p. 78). What is unpleasure and alien is located as external to the ego: "what was abolished internally returns from without" (p. 71). In his paper on negation there is an emphasis on the mechanism of expulsion.

Bion (1958) drew a distinction between psychotic and hysterical hallucinations. This difference is related directly to an increase in the patient's capacity to tolerate depression. The psychotic hallucination contains elements analogous to part-objects; the hysterical hallucination contains whole objects and is associated with depression.

I would suggest that another differentiation may be that whereas the conflict for the psychotic is between life and death, in the hysterical hallucination it is between love and hate. Both, I believe, contain aspects of remembering. Might it be that Carolina moved between the two? Whereas the hallucination of the knife belonged more to the psychotic part of her personality, with the lurking possibility of murder, might the human-sized wasp belong more to the hysterical register? The wasp was clearly an association to an object, to her mother, to me, and to herself. Some analytic work took place during the time between the two that had transformed the images into words, from the lethal possibility of murder to the experience of more potentially controlled danger.

De Masi, Davalli, Giustino, and Pergami (2015) have indicated that in hallucinations there is a withdrawal from external reality into a sensorial mode. One is dealing with pure sensoriality that has not reached representation or symbolization (Segal, 1957). According to these authors "during the hallucinatory experience, the patient does not think, he *sees* or *feels*" (De Masi et al., 2015, p. 313, italics in original). They also quote from Perceval, for whom the hallucinatory state requires a position of passive acquiescence (p. 308). I can relate this idea to an aspect of Carolina's experience of compliance throughout her life.

Green has suggested that in the treatment of non-neurotic patients, one is dealing not with an economy of unconscious desire, but with a "logic of despair" (Urribarri, 2013, p. 21). This logic is less organized than that of the primary process and has to contend with unprocessed elements coming from the id. Thinking is dominated by the work of the negative (Green, 1999). The aim of the analytic work is to transform hallucinations into words that create a narrative about the patient's history, transforming delirium into play and death into absence.

In the case of such patients, it is a failure of hallucinatory wish-fulfilment that is the basic model for an understanding of the psyche. This failure is the outcome of a traumatic encounter with the primary object. It is not possible to invest the mnemic trace, because of the pain or terror that it will provoke. Rather than evoking an experience of pleasure, it is an experience of distress that comes to the fore. Psychic reality is decathected; the patient withdraws into a "personal, bodily and sensory space of his own" (Urribarri, 2013, p. 293). Mental functioning becomes restricted, cutting off more mature functions. Words are treated as things, as Freud suggested in his paper on the Unconscious. The patient is not present in her own discourse and in the session; she also feels like a prisoner. Passivation, the process whereby the patient submits herself to the analytic care, is almost impossible (Green, 1986a).

Paul Williams has written about patients who have suffered an experience of "incorporation of an invasive object", a primitive introjection of aspects of an object, which creates an experience of inundation that can give rise to personality disturbance (Williams, 2004).[8] He refers to this process as a form of "proto-identification" that takes place in early infancy and expresses a failure of containment and maternal alpha-function (Bion, 1962b). The infant incorporates these violent projections as part of his own mental representational system, and normal identification processes are disrupted. An impairment of the development of the sense of self takes place. The outcome of the early trauma undergone by such patients is expressed in "an amalgam of inchoate experiences, the residuum or precipitate of which may correspond to the 'foreign body' experience lodged in the Unconscious and in the body and which lacks mental representational status" (Williams, 2004, p. 1342). Here I have suggested that the production of the images that take on a hallucinatory form become an achievement of the analysis, at the origin of representation of such experiences.

There is an intrinsic link between the framing structure as the place for symbolization and the analytic experience that will reproduce aspects of the patient's experience with the primary object. The framing structure is not perceptible as such, but only through the productions that it gives rise to in the setting (Green, 1999). It is in the *après-coup* of an analysis that one has access to the traces left by the traumatic, archaic past, some of which will find representation for the first time in the here-and-now of the analytic process (Perelberg, 2006, 2007, 2011, 2015).

This leads me to underline an aspect of any analytic treatment, which is its dramatic dimension. Since Breuer and Freud's statement that hysterics suffer mainly from reminiscences (Freud, 1895d) and Freud's work "Remembering, Repeating and Working-Through" (1914g), the idea that psychic conflicts can be expressed in ways other than words has become familiar in psychoanalysis. At this point in their work, however, Freud and Breuer saw the symptom as a repetition of the past. Later, Freud was to understand the phenomenon of transference more fully in terms of the links between the there-and-then and the here-and-now. Transference is overdetermined—like Proust's madeleine, which emerges out of a phenomenon of metaphoric and metonymic irradiation, associating several moments, places and memories and ultimately expressing the infantile desire of the narrator himself (Kristeva, 1996; Perelberg, 2008a).

It is my belief that the analytic situation has a dramatic dimension and is, by definition, traumatic because it evokes the state of helplessness of the new-born infant (*Hilflosigkeit*), which is the prototype of the traumatic situation and at the origin of the experience of anxiety (Perelberg, 2007). It is in this context that the relationship with the primordial object is brought forth.

Transference is filled with our patients' desires, which are linked to their unconscious phantasies, and infantile sexuality, ruled now by the compulsion to repeat.

In his *Introductory Lectures on Psycho-Analysis*, Freud had already stated that, in traumatic neurosis,

> patients regularly repeat the traumatic situation in their dreams; where hysteriform attacks occur that admit of an analysis, we find that the attack corresponds to a complete transplanting of the patient into the traumatic situation. It is as though these patients had not finished with the traumatic situation, as though they were still faced by it as an immediate task which has not been dealt with.
>
> (Freud, 1916–17, p. 274)

In *Beyond the Pleasure Principle*, when briefly discussing traumatic dreams, Freud postulates:

> Now dreams occurring in traumatic neuroses have the characteristic of repeatedly bringing the patient back into the situation of his accident, a situation from which he wakes up in another fright.
>
> (Freud, 1920g, p. 13)

Under the register of the compulsion to repeat, the original traumatic situation is being lived again in dreams in the present (see also Perelberg, 2000). Later (1933a) Freud will say that these traumatic dreams generate anxiety.

In 1920 there was, therefore, an important substitution in Freud's model, an emphasis on representations being replaced by one on the act (Green, 2002a, p. 163). These ideas are specifically relevant to a modern conceptualization of the analytic situation and the understanding that patients act rather than remember.

The repetition of traumatic situations is a characteristic not only of traumatic dreams, but of any dreams, and of the analytic situation itself. One is no longer referring to a setting wherein the patient speaks and the analyst interprets, but to a dramatic encounter wherein patient and analyst will minimally repeat an interaction that is relevant to the patient's past.[9] The challenge for any analysis is to introduce a transformation in the narrative anticipated by the compulsion to repeat.

Further developments

Five years into the analysis, Carolina met a man, married, and became pregnant. In the initial months of her pregnancy her sense of persecution increased, but things changed when she was able to see the first scan. The baby became a living human being for her, and at this point her dreams took on a more human quality. Carolina became progressively more excited about the pregnancy.

P: The changes in my body feel mysterious and magical. I never imagined I'd feel all right in this way. I am hoping that all these changes that are happening are so that I can breast-feed. I am sure that I can feel this way because I am coming here.

A: Perhaps you came to analysis in order to be able to have a baby.

The dream from the beginning of her analysis came to my mind: the mother who announces death and also the words "against abortion". Carolina could perhaps now see herself as a mother who wanted to be life-giving, not an announcer of death.

Notes

1 "I make the assumption that the child (whatever culture he is born into) is held by the mother against her body. When contact with the mother's body is broken, what remains of this experience is the trace of bodily contact—as a rule the mother's arms—which constitutes a framing structure sheltering the loss of the perception of the maternal object, *in the form of a negative hallucination of it*" (Green, 2005b, p. 161, italics in original).

2 "Are we not justified in inferring that the negative hallucination of the mother, without in any way representing anything, has made the conditions for representation possible" (Green, 2001, p. 86)?

3 It is crucial to distinguish the negative hallucination of the mother as the requirement for normal processes of development from what may be understood as a negative hallucination of thought that refers to states of emptiness and holes in the psyche, as in borderline structures (see also Pirlot & Cupa, 2012, pp. 57–59). The negative hallucination of the mother, at the beginnings of psychic life, is to be distinguished from the negative hallucination of the object in terms of the denial of its existence, an expression of foreclosure. One is distinguishing the role of the negative in its structuring function from its destructive aspects (see Perelberg, 2016a). Freud stated in 1917: "I may add … that any attempt to explain hallucination would have to start out from the negative rather than positive hallucination" (1917d, p. 232).

4 Film precis: Alice Barlow is murdered by an unknown man, who then ransacks her house, looking for her famous valuable rubies. The house remains empty for years, until newlyweds Paul and Bella Mallen move in. Bella soon finds herself misplacing small objects, and before long Paul has her believing that she is losing her sanity. B. G. Rough, a former detective involved in the original murder investigation, immediately suspects him of Alice Barlow's murder. Paul uses the gas lamps to search the closed-off upper floors, which causes the lamps in the rest of the house to dim slightly. When Bella comments on this, he tells her she is imagining things. Bella is persuaded she is hearing noises, unaware that Paul enters the upper floors from the house next-door. This is part of a larger pattern of deception to which Bella is subjected. It is revealed that Paul is the wanted Louis Bauer, who has returned to the house to search for the rubies he was unable to find after the murder [https://en.wikipedia.org/wiki/Gaslight_(1940_film)]. "Gaslighting" describes a form of psychological abuse in which the victim is gradually manipulated into doubting his or her own sanity. The term originates from the 1938 stage play *Gaslight,* by Patrick Hamilton, and its two film adaptations.

5 "I was playing in the garden near my nurse and was carving with my pocket-knife in the bark of one of the walnut-trees that come into my dream as well. Suddenly, to my unspeakable terror, I noticed that I had cut through the little finger of my (right or left?) hand, so that it was only hanging on by its skin. I felt no pain, but great fear. I did not venture to say anything to my nurse, who was only a few paces distant, but I sank down on the nearest seat and sat there incapable of casting another glance at my finger. At last I calmed down, took a look at the finger, and saw that it was entirely uninjured" (Freud, 1914a, p. 205).

6 In this text Freud attempts to distinguish between "dementia praecox", which produces violent hallucinations, and paranoia, which employs projection. He suggests that dementia praecox indicates a point of fixation between auto-erotism and object love, whereas paranoia indicates a regression to the state of narcissism. Freud concludes, however, that paranoid and schizophrenic phenomena may be combined in different proportions. In the Schreber case, he suggests, one can identify the production of hallucinations and distinguish it from the paranoid mechanisms of projection (Freud, 1911c, pp. 77–78).

7 Some other clinical examples that illustrate the terror of this archaic mother may be found in Perelberg (1995, 1997c, 1999b, 2003, 2015).

8 In *Studies on Hysteria* (1895d), Freud refers to the traumatic thus: "We presume that the psychical trauma—or more precisely the memory of the trauma *acts like a foreign body* which long after its entry must be continued to be regarded as an agent that is still at work" (p. 6; italics added). Freud is pointing out the way in which what is traumatic is unabsorbable by representation and inaccessible to symbolization.

9 This is the paradigmatic shift introduced by Freud with his *Beyond the Pleasure Principle* (1920g) and "Constructions in Analysis" (1937d). In the British Psychoanalytical Society, key papers that have continued to explore these fundamental issues include those by Heimann (1950), Sandler (1976), Segal (1977), King (1978), and Joseph (1985). Sandler has delineated the various stages of development of the concept of projective identification. With Klein, it refers to a process that takes place in phantasy. A second stage may be identified with the developments described in the work of Heimann (1950), Racker (1968), and Grinberg (1962), whereby the countertransference reaction on the part of the analyst becomes a possible source of information about what is occurring in the mind of the patient. In the work of Bion, this extension of the understanding of the concept finds expression in his concepts of the container and reverie: what is projected onto the analyst is contained and transformed by the work of reverie on the part of the analyst. A fourth stage may be found in the work of Sandler himself (1976) and of Joseph (1985), both of whom indicate how what is projected onto the analyst provokes a response in the analyst, who is "nudged" to respond in a certain way (see also Spillius, 1992). In what concerns dreams, Kohon (2000) has suggested that these may be a form of acting out. Perelberg has suggested that "dreams contain a condensed narrative about the transference relationship and encapsulate a narrative that will unfold as the analysis progresses" (2000, p. 109).

4

LOVE AND MELANCHOLIA IN THE ANALYSIS OF WOMEN BY WOMEN

Introduction

In this chapter I suggest that in the analysis of women by women analysts, one may be confronted by a melancholic core in the relationship to an internal maternal imago. The attachment to this primary love object may be preserved in a melancholic, invisible way and reach representation only in the *après-coup* of the analytic process. It is my suggestion that attacks on the body that take place in the course of such an analysis are expressions of the attacks on this primary object, at the same time as this object is preserved in oneself.

These analyses bring to the fore intense somatic experiences that tend to be expressed in fragmented, part-object terms, so that what emerges in the analysis are bodily parts, such as the breasts, uterus, ovaries, and anus (see Cournut-Janin, 1998). The process of bodily fragmentation that takes place makes it difficult at times to recognize whether one is dealing with a hysterical presentation or with melancholia. The differentiation will be brought out—as is demonstrated in this chapter—in the analyst's countertransference, so that the issue at stake is experienced by the analyst not in terms of a battle between love and hate but, more accurately, in terms of life and death. The experience is that the very life of the patient may be under threat.

The pre-oedipal relationship to the mother was a later discovery in Freud's work. He referred to the archaic relationship of the little girl to her mother as a "dark continent", difficult to access in analysis because it belongs to the pre-verbal, sensorial domain;[1] he hoped that women analysts would be more able to shed light on these processes. Freud nevertheless identified the little girl's sexual longings towards the mother and the wish to give her a baby.

Recently Julia Kristeva has suggested a psychosomatic fatigue present in women that expresses her inability "to choose the sex of her object of desire, because she has failed to work through her bisexuality" (2012, p. 115). Women are in the impossible positions of wanting their mothers and their fathers in one and the same love object. This constitutes an inherent bisexuality in women in that the love for the mother is never given up.

I believe that melancholia may be encountered in the analysis of women and that it is potentially intensified in the analysis of women by women analysts.

Melancholia, in contrast to mourning, is characterized by the experience of the individual not consciously knowing what has been lost; it is related, in some way, to an object-loss that is withdrawn from consciousness. It is my suggestion that it is only in the analytic process that the lost primary erotic object will be found and constituted in the vicissitudes of the transference and countertransference.

Freud also states that "in mourning it is the world which has become poor and empty; in melancholia it is the ego itself" (1917e, p. 246); the patient represents his ego to us as worthless. This, Freud explains, is due to ambivalence. The analysis of a melancholic patient may thus lead to potential impasses that could give rise to a sadomasochistic relationship in the analysis.

There are interconnected ideas in this thinking:

1. The attachment to the lost primary object is preserved in a melancholic, invisible way, and the longing to which it is connected might reach representation only in the *après-coup* of the analytic process. The links between this primary love, melancholia, and the unrepresentable in analyses of women, as well as their representation reached through the vicissitudes of the transference and countertransference, are explored further in this chapter.
2. There is an attempt in many of these analyses to organize such inchoate, at times frightening, bodily experiences into a sadomasochistic relationship with the female analyst. The

sadomasochism and the suffering that it entails is, however, secondary to the melancholy that such experiences mask. This perspective raises profound questions of technique in that interpretations that focus on the destructive function of the sadistic attacks—on the self and other—may miss the underlying longings that these attacks conceal. Green identified a crucial point of technique: "to interpret hatred in structures which take on depressive characteristics amounts to never approaching the primary core of this constellation" (1986b, p. 146). This echoes something that Riviere herself had stated: "Nothing will lead more surely to a negative therapeutic reaction in the patient than failure to recognize anything but the aggression in his material" (1936, p. 310).

3. The somatic in psychoanalysis must include unconscious phantasies about the body. This perspective evokes what Freud referred to as the mysterious leap from the psychic into the somatic, which was the foundation of psychoanalysis in the studies of hysteria. In psychoanalysis, the somatic is intrinsically linked to the sexual and includes infantile phantasy life.
4. The somatic is indissolubly linked to the primary relationship to the maternal object.

Hypothesis: the core conflict and bodily symptoms

It is perhaps not surprising that so many women's struggle to turn away and separate from their mothers involves a bodily symptom. Most of the analyses described in *Female Experience: Three Generations of Women Analysts on Work with Women* (Raphael-Leff & Perelberg, 1997; see also Raphael-Leff & Perelberg, 2008) involved a bodily symptom. Thus, Enid Balint suggested that a woman needs to feel that she was satisfied by her mother's body as an infant in order to feel that her own body satisfied her mother (Perelberg, 1997a, p. 29). Balint described the way in which her two women patients' sexuality was an expression of their relationship to their mothers (Balint, 1997). Burgner (1997) discussed the analysis of a 17-year-old bulimic girl who had attempted suicide. For her patient, Cara, bingeing and vomiting were her only possession and her way of separating from her mother, whom she experienced as intrusive and invasive. Mother and daughter were bound to each other through a crazy and addictive sexuality. The transference–countertransference was an important source of information about the patient's affective states and one that allowed the patient's pre-verbal states of mind to be understood in the process. Birksted-Breen discussed the case of an anorexic patient in terms of "her wish for, and fear of, fusion with her mother" (1989, p. 30). She suggested that in the anorexic patient there is a disturbance in the area of symbolization, which does not allow a space to be developed between mother and daughter. Whereas in the boy this conflict might lead to a perversion, in the case of her patient it led to anorexia as an attempt to have a body that was different from her mother's (Birksted-Breen, 1989). She quotes Boris, who discusses fusion in terms of a "not me" and "not you" space (Boris, 1984, p. 319) and suggests that the anorexic girl fails to maintain a transitional space in the relationship to her mother.

My patient "Maria" developed a series of bodily symptoms in the course of her analysis. I understood the convulsive twitching that she showed throughout many months on the couch as "the concrete experience of her contact with me, where she felt both excited and attacked by me". They expressed her experience of a maternal intrusion that felt murderous in the transference, as well as her bodily discharge of her murderous and erotic feelings towards me (Perelberg, 1997a, p. 24; 1997b; see also Perelberg, 2016d).

In my Introduction (Perelberg, 1997a) to *Female Experience*, I then suggested that many of the bodily experiences of some women seen in clinical practice represent attempts to have a body and a sense of self that are separate from the mother's. At the same time, these symptoms seem to represent an aspect of the relationship with the mother that has not been properly internalized: this is the mother as protector against the child's own sexual and destructive phantasies.

What is also a source of struggle is the primary erotic and ambivalent relationship to the mother. Symptoms may have a paradoxical function, thus expressing the conflict between longing for and fear of fusion with the mother. The girl, says Irigaray, "has the mother, in some sense, in her skin, in the humidity of the mucous membranes, in the intimacy of her most intimate parts, in the mystery of her relation to gestation, birth and to her sexual identity" (1989, p. 133). This is the conflict at the core of perversions that Glasser has discussed (1979), but it may have a wider relevance, as being found at the core of each individual's relationship with her or his mother. It is my suggestion that this pre-oedipal pull is more prevalent in the analysis of women by women analysts. Although some of the cases discussed in that book may seem extreme, I would suggest that they highlight some of the archaic forms of the little girl's relationship to her mother. In my experience, it is not uncommon that the analyses of women by women involve bodily symptoms. Is it that in her conflict between identification with and differentiation from her mother's body, the woman will locate her conflict in her own body? Is this in contrast with boys, for whom the conflict is externalized? In previous work I contrasted the hysteria of Breuer's patient, Anna O, with the violence of the patient whom I then named Karl. I then asked: "Is it that Anna O's attacks in her own body the body of her mother, whereas Karl has to find in the other, the (m)other?" (Perelberg, 1999b, p. 186).

Freud was the first to point out, in 1920, the relevance of the analyst's gender, when treating a female homosexual who developed a negative transference to him (1920a). Later, in 1931, he also emphasized the importance of the ability of women analysts to gain more access to the pre-oedipal transference in female patients (1931b). It has been women analysts who have mostly written about the analysis of women in a way that takes into account their gender and sexuality in the transference (Perelberg, 1997a, 2008b). Why should that be? Might it be that a bodily identification is more easily available in the analysis of women by women analysts as their bodies resemble each other? This raises interesting questions about the way in which the body of the analyst might be internalized at the perceptive level and reach representation as a framing structure in the course of an analysis (Perelberg, 2015, 2016d).

Many analysts have suggested that the sequence of material presented in the transference may reflect the sex of the therapist, early pre-oedipal material being more frequently identified in analyses with female analysts. Glover (1955), Blum (1971), Pines (1993), and Balint (1973) also point out in their work with female patients that there are specific issues that arise in the transference to female analysts. Pines believes that "a woman analyst's physical capacity to be a mother appears to facilitate the transference of primitive feelings arising from partial maternal deprivation" (1993, p. 24).

This is in contrast with the transference to male analysts, which often tends to be reported as presenting itself in an erotized pseudo-heterosexual way.

In all this, one must not lose sight of the eminently oedipal configuration of the analytic situation. Chasseguet-Smirgel (1986) has pointed out that in analysis the analysand is offered a womb, a potential for regression, but in the setting itself, with its framework and rules, the limits are also indicated, in the same way as the father separates the mother and the child. She discusses the issue in terms of how the femininity of analysts—whether male or female—affects their professional practice. I have come to think, nevertheless, that there is a powerful pull in the analysis of women patients by women analysts for the pre-oedipal domain to express itself more vividly.

The following clinical case illustrates a five-times-a week analysis.

Clinical vignette: "Emma"

Emma came to analysis in her early twenties because of her constant and intense anxiety, which had a paralysing effect on her life. She came from a Latin American country, and the analysis was carried out in her mother tongue. Emma had an exacerbated preoccupation with her body and experienced different kinds of transient ailments that tended to abate when anxiety subsided. She was also extremely anxious at the first consultation and could not decide whether she wanted to come to see me again. Looking at the books in my consulting room, she was concerned that I would not have a space for her in my mind—a transferential expression of her relationship to her father, a famous novelist, who, she felt, had not had a space in his mind for her, especially after her mother died. Emma had experienced her father as more focused on his older son, who had followed in his footsteps and was also a well-known writer.

Emma came for several consultations before she was able to decide to come for analysis, and she was reluctant to lie on the couch. After a few months of sitting on a chair facing me, she eventually did lie on the couch and started a five-times-a-week analytic process. In the very first dream she brought after lying on the couch, I had joined her and we were locked in an erotic embrace. That first dream, after she had been reluctant to lie on the couch, alerted me to the pull of the erotic pre-oedipal domain that she felt that she had to protect herself from.

The first years of Emma's analysis were dominated by accounts of the traumatic events of her life. As a young child, she had had a very close relationship with her mother and remembered wanting to follow her everywhere. Her mother seemed to have been very dedicated and loving to both her children. She had been a pianist until before her children were born but had retired after their birth and only performed occasionally. The family lived in a large city in Latin America. They constituted a small family, as neither parent had a sibling. They spent their weekends at a farm two hours away that had been in the mother's family for many generations. It was at this farm that her mother had a horse-riding accident when Emma was very young, broke her spine, and died a few weeks later. This took place during a week of holidays, when Emma and her mother were alone on the farm. Her brother was away, spending time with their paternal grandfather. Emma had tried frantically to reach someone to help her, but she felt it had taken a long time before she was eventually able to reach an adult. Her experience was that they were very distant from the dramatic situation in which she was immersed. Knowing this now enabled me to understand the experience that was so pervasive in the consulting room for quite some time: a frantic, ever-present anxiety, a sense of a catastrophe that was always in the process of happening. I put this forward to the patient in the following interpretation:

> "The experience is of a catastrophe that has already happened but is, nevertheless, always happening."

This (open) interpretation (Perelberg, 2003, p. 590) linked her constant state of anxiety to the experience that had preceded her mother's death and her experience of being left with no help. Our subsequent work centred on this event and led to a long period of calm and development in Emma's life. She married, had two babies, and undertook a postgraduate academic course. I often had the thought that Emma had not had a mother to witness her development as a teenager and young woman, and I felt very moved by her achievements.

A few years later, as I raised the theme of ending of the treatment, Emma developed a series of bodily sensations—palpitations that evoked fears of a heart attack, as well as various other worrying and undefined symptoms. A dramatic weight loss in the space of a few weeks raised the fear of cancer, which led to tests, the results of which were all negative. She described them as feelings with no thought. She undertook a series of medical investigations by endocrinologists, neurologists, and gynaecologists, all of whom consistently told her that there was nothing physically wrong with her. Eventually, after a few months, the sensations concentrated on her vagina. These were described at great length throughout her sessions. For many months, I experienced a sense of helplessness as I listened to detailed accounts of Emma's experiences and trips to see doctors—mainly men—and of her bodily sensations. I experienced myself as very supportive during this period and made just a few attempts to interpret these symptoms as part of a symbolic chain.

It seemed to me that my suggestion that we should end the analysis had evoked the fear of trauma and death and a powerful repetition of her inner state of anxiety and fear after her mother's accident and during the period of some weeks that preceded her death. Throughout the ensuing months of her analysis, I was deeply concerned about her state of health. Progressively, as the various medical doctors could find nothing wrong with her, I became more certain that this had been a reaction to my suggestion that we should begin to think about a date to end the analysis. It was more possible to offer tentative interpretations that addressed psychic meaning.

The following session took place towards the end of this period:

Thursday

Emma comes in on time and lies on the couch.

She tells me at the beginning of the session about a letter from the neurologist, which he had sent to her GP earlier in the month.

PATIENT: I am going to see him tomorrow. He also said that if the situation deteriorates, he will undertake further investigations. I don't want any more tests; I don't want any more doctors. I am afraid of going to sleep, as I don't know what will happen during the night …

I had this dream last night: I can see the visual image of it extremely clearly. *I went to the hairdresser. There was a most horrible scene. There were all these women, lying on their backs—like in a beauty salon, or also a dental chair. They were all naked, quite old, with no skin; you could see their muscles, their flesh. It reminded me of a kind of art exhibit, where they were showing dead bodies. There were, then, these eight women lying in a morgue, having their relaxed treatment. On one woman one could see all her veins—it is a shame I can't have a snapshot of it for you to see.* [I had a vivid image of what she was describing that felt horrific.] *There was some kind of emphasis on the pelvic area. They were all so old. At my hairdresser's, I meet quite a lot of old women.*

When I went to do one of my tests a few weeks ago, I saw a woman like the one in the dream. This was a disturbing dream. It was a shock to look at these bodies. They were very taut. One image I have in mind is of the torso. There was no bleeding. They were intact bodies without skin. I had a funny incident—not funny, really. When I went home, I put a key in my door and could not open the door. I assumed someone must have left and had locked it from the inside. I was feeling cold and tired. I thought that it would be less expensive if I broke a pane on the back door. I was going to do that, but I decided to try the lock once more and was able to open the door.

[Silence.]

A: I feel this dream is occupying my head … It was such a horrific dream … Perhaps this is what you are afraid will happen in the night if you go to sleep; you will have such a horrific dream.

P: Exactly! I feel despairing.

A: I wonder if the dream expresses the experience of coming here for all these eight years: the confusion between the dental chair, the hairdressing salon, the tests, and the morgue. It is a horrific experience at the moment; you feel exposed, fragile, without a skin, and frightened that we will not have the key to open that door …

[I was also thinking about the presence in the background, throughout all these years, of the body of the patient's dead mother.]

P: I am terrified of having to do a lumbar puncture or a spinal test … I agree about the dream; it is so shocking, this whole idea. All we talk about now is my body, and my vagina and my veins.

A: Yet you were able to open the door and go in ...

P: All I do is to talk about my sick body. I have no doubt that there is a disturbance of sensation in that area [the vagina]. It makes me want to cry ...

A: Perhaps it feels safer to talk in the language of symptoms, even if it is, at the same time, so upsetting ...

[Silence.]

P: ... But I am so worried about it all. I am totally convinced that there is something wrong with my body. I cannot believe that my psyche would have the power to provoke all this.

One could see the beginnings of Emma's capacity to open the door to a way of thinking about her bodily experiences. The depicting of the dead bodies in the dream was horrific; it conveyed, via very distressing images, what had felt impossible to put into words—the way she felt dead inside, in identification with the dead mother. It also conveyed my struggle, over the last few months, to keep herself as a live analyst who would be able to offer a dialogue that would facilitate the emergence of a lively woman. Yet there was also a door that was starting to be opened. The end of the session indicates how tentative all this was—opening the door felt like something almost impossible, and Emma went back to her despair about her bodily symptoms.

A few weeks later, Emma described the events surrounding the death of a neighbour who, she was told, had lived in the house next door to her all her life and only left there to be buried. She described the coffin being taken away in great detail.

When thinking about this neighbour, who just left his house, dead, I found myself saying:

> "This makes me think about the experience of the last few months; we have both lived inside your vagina; we cannot escape from this experience, or give any meaning to it. We just have to be there, until one of us dies."

She stopped for a while, surprised, and then became immersed in her thoughts, quiet, until the end of the session. I was myself surprised at this interpretation, which conveyed so much my experience with Emma over the last few months.

Whereas up to now she had kept telling the analyst that there were no thoughts connected to her various bodily sensations, progressively she was able to relate more about conscious fantasies. These included scenes between women. Four of these scenes were especially disturbing to her, and she described them in detail, hesitantly, and with a very real sense of shame/excitement.

Emma sounded despairing: as these were recent fantasies, was she becoming a homosexual after all this analysis?

I thought that all the stages of libidinal investment in the relationship with her mother/analyst were present in these scenes—from the surface of the skin to the oral, anal, and phallic dimensions. I said to her that these scenes expressed the various ways of penetrating/being penetrated by a woman through all possible orifices and surfaces of the body. These were also ways of preserving that woman. Emma felt immensely relieved.

The sequence of the sexual scenes between women that she described seemed to constitute a somatic/erotic memory/phantasy of her relationship to her mother/analyst, evoking Emma's infantile memories of the different ways of incorporating her mother and her body.

There followed a period when Emma described memories of bodily contact with her mother that expressed the nature of her passionate attachment to her mother as a child: burying her face in her big breasts, hugging her, sitting on her lap, smelling her buttocks when showering together when she was little and her head only reached that height. These different memories had now become eroticized, leaving her feeling bewildered and frightened, at the mercy of a tidal wave that seemed to destroy all the existing barriers and protectors erected by repression. Through the memories of her exploration of the mystery of her mother's body and sexuality, it is her own sexuality as a woman that Emma is seeking to understand in the here and now of her analysis.

This phase of Emma's analysis was lived out by both of us as a real trauma that was being repeated over and over. Each memory/phantasy felt like a "coup" (blows, trauma), potentially developing into symptoms that were felt in each part of her body, and one could not be sure whether the analysis would eventually lead to working through in a process of *après-coup*, or whether it would continue to be just a repetition of the trauma. In the many symptoms that Emma experienced during this period of the analysis it was unclear whether she was, indeed, physically ill, or whether eventually her symptoms could be understood as part of a symbolic chain. Paradoxically, this thought enabled me to feel myself freer of her symptoms.

After many months of agony, confusion, and symptoms, the analysis progressively moved into a different phase: one of dreams, associations, and working through. Emma's symptoms gradually disappeared. Eventually, two years later, she was able to take on an academic position, and she started to write. A process of identification with her father and the analytic function came to the fore. This analytic function enabled her to emerge from an enmeshed identification with her mother, and a real work of mourning started to take place. The image of her mother itself became a livelier presence in her mind.

The encounter with the melancholic feminine in the analysis of women

Freud states that in melancholia there is an identification of the ego with the abandoned object.

> Thus, the shadow of the object fell upon the ego, and the latter could henceforth be judged by a special agency, as though it were an object, the forsaken object. In this way, an object-loss was transformed into an ego-loss and the conflict between the ego and the loved person into a cleavage between the critical activity of the ego and the ego as altered by identification.
>
> (Freud, 1917e, p. 249)

The loss of the object leads to its incorporation within the ego, and this, in turn, becomes a way of taking possession of the object. Incorporation has bodily emphases—in contrast with identification, which requires the relinquishment of the object. Torok has suggested that the term "incorporation" applies to a loss that occurred "before the desires concerning the object might have been freed" (1994, p. 112). This loss acts as a prohibition, and "the prohibited object is settled in the ego in order to compensate for the lost pleasure and the failed introjection" (p. 113). Torok suggests that incorporation may occur by means of representations, affects, or bodily states. While introjection ends dependency on the object, incorporation reinforces the imaginary ties to the object (p. 114).

Judith Kestenberg proposed a distinction between "inner" and "outer" anatomical configurations and the associated phantasies (1968). The little girl's representation of her genitals as an inner space has an impact on her experience of her femininity. Kestenberg' s views have been very influential among French analysts, who have indicated the relevance of the construction of inner space in the sequence of women's development, from being in the womb and then being held in the mother's arms, to the construction of the potential inner space from the mouth to the anus and, finally, to the vagina, leading eventually to the actual inner space of the woman's womb in pregnancy and its externalization during childbirth (Cournut-Janin, 1998; Kristeva, 1995; see also Brierley, 1932). The three orifices (mouth, anus, vagina) as well as the sensory surface of the skin, working as a boundary, comprise the main ways that women progressively experience inner space (see also Chasseguet-Smirgel, 1976). It was as if, through Emma's breakdown into sensorial, bodily experiences, she was structuring her feminine body in her analysis. The encounter with the feminine in an analysis may be a voyage into that which characterizes the unconscious itself: disruption, discontinuity, and incoherence (e.g., Abraham & Torok, 1994).

The middle phase of Emma's analysis plunged the analytic couple into a somatic universe made up of bodily parts: breasts, uterus, ovaries, anus, and vagina. They were living in a domain of somatic confusion, fragmentation, and suffering, plunged into a massive regressive movement, in a process of rupture with anything that it was possible to think about: the emphases were on bodily sensations that were overwhelming and experienced as lethal.

Monique and Jean Cournut (Cournut-Janin & Cournut, 1993) have referred to a type of transference in the analysis of women as an archaic memory of a maternal imago that gives the impression that the analytic work meets "dead bodies"—the residue of mortal combat. Their description is very evocative of my experience with Emma in this middle phase: that of being involved in a deadly battle, where one does not know whether the patient or the analysis will survive—a confusion between life and death. This is also the description of the pre-oedipal domain to which one can only have access within the framework of an analysis.

Emma had suffered a particular trauma in her life, losing her mother so early. It is my experience, nevertheless, that what we had access to in her analysis are the pre-oedipal elements that are present in the analysis of many women by women analysts.

Kristeva (2000) describes the pre-oedipal as a play of bodily rhythms and prelinguistic exchanges between infant and mother: it is the domain of the semiotic. She refers to what Plato, in the *Timaeus*, called the chora as the site of the undifferentiated bodily space that mother and child share. With the Oedipus complex, the symbolic—the domain of unified texts, cultural representations, and knowledge—is dominant. This distinction between the semiotic and the symbolic is, however, retrospective, as it is only through the symbolic that one has access to the semiotic. For Kristeva, subjectivity is founded on a constitutive repression of the maternal, the chora, the semiotic, the abject (liminal states, like pregnancy). Perhaps one could say that in this analysis we accessed the experience of the abject, a potential disintegration of the body into bodily parts, before a process of reintegration could take place.

Kristeva suggests a two-sided Oedipus phase for the girl: "Oedipus 1" relates to both boys and girls, where the desire for the mother is dominant, before there is a change of the object for the girl towards the father:

> Masturbation, incestuous desire for the mother: here is the first aspect of the Oedipus complex (I will call it Oedipus 1) that structurally defines the girl, as well as the boy, before she arrives at Oedipus 2, which causes her to change objects (the father instead of the mother). Yet, starting with this structuring (Oedipus 1), there are differences between the girl's phallicism and the boy's.
>
> (Kristeva, 2000, p. 99)

Kristeva emphasizes women's inherent bisexuality in that the passion for the mother is never given up. They are destined to continue to desire their mother, and this characterizes their fundamental *étrangeté*. Kristeva refers to the woman's endogenous homosexuality (2012, p. 117), which "remains the repressed center of feminine psychosexuality throughout the life of the subject, just as inaccessible to analysis as 'the rock of castration', if not more so" (p. 117). Women are in the impossible position of desiring both their mothers and their fathers in one and the same love object. Kristeva suggests that the cause of women's extravagance is their inherent bisexuality (Oliver, 2012). "The female subject [is subjected] to an eternal psychosexual incompletion: tiring, exhausting hesitation between unstable, undecidable objects of desire (as 'marked psychic bisexuality requires')" (Kristeva, 2012, p. 120). In this formulation, Kristeva follows Freud, for whom "bisexuality … comes to the fore more clearly in women than men" (1931b, p. 227).[2]

Kristeva believes that in psychoanalytic treatment a woman can move through the borderline state that is her inherent bisexuality towards "serenity". This serenity actually explodes the illusion of oneness and wholeness in order to love passionately and yet let go of that love to embrace life.

Melancholia and eroticization

From the above, one can identify a crucial dimension that is present in the analyses of these female patients: a struggle with a melancholic core that cannot be elaborated (for the way in which this melancholia may also be found eroticized in the analysis of a man, see Perelberg, 2011). The core of melancholia is the murder of the primordial object that is lost for ever, yet in a way is never entirely lost, because the subject will always be attempting to find it again. It is this object that was never possessed that these female patients try to recover through apparent sadism and cruelty towards their objects and, in their analysis, towards their own bodies and towards the analyst.

> If the love for the object—a love which cannot be given up though the object itself is given up—takes refuge in narcissistic identification, then the hate comes into operation on this substitutive object, abusing it, debasing it, making it suffer and deriving sadistic satisfaction from its suffering.
>
> (Freud, 1917e, p. 250)

This quotation establishes a link between melancholia, sadism, masochism, and the negative therapeutic reaction in which the patient "refuses" to get better. This would mean letting the maternal object go. It was, indeed, when I referred to the possible ending of the analysis that this period that I have been describing was precipitated. The experience in the countertransference during this phase of the analysis is that of inutility, an expression of the power of the forces of narcissism. The analyst is required to relive in the process the same fate as the lost/destroyed object. I cannot overemphasize the despair that I felt about whether Emma would survive and emerge in a more "serene" way from her analysis. I struggled with whether it was ethical to continue, as Emma seemed to be getting worse rather than better. Throughout this whole period, however, she never missed a session and always lay on the couch. This left me, at the same time, with a profound sense of a working alliance between us that underlined the whole experience.

Towards the end of the second phase of her analysis, Emma brought another dream: She was in a bathtub, and there were lots of tubes coming out of her, including her mouth. She was being fed in this way, somewhere between life and death. The memory was that of her mother on her deathbed. But the tubes also reminded her of recent examinations of her genitals, where the injection of a contrasting liquid left her with burning sensations.

The equation is present between the mouth and the genitals, the feeding situation and excitation, life and death; my comment to Emma was as follows:

> "On the couch, there is a confusion between life-giving nourishment, sexual excitation, and death."

Après-coup

Emma's analysis illustrates the issue of repetition linked with the sexual and the traumatic, the fractality present in the *après-coup* (Chervet, 2009; Perelberg, 2006, 2015). A fractal is a complex geometric structure the properties of which repeat themselves: an image contains a smaller copy of itself, the sequence appearing to recur infinitely. The repetitions, however, reflect the structure, exactly like mirrors that reflect each other to infinity. At one point in the analysis, Emma had the following dream:

> *A man had come to install a special kind of mouthwash in the bathroom—it looked like some kind of hotel bathroom, with a huge dispenser, with lots of loops. It had a mirror. I also wondered why there were so many mirrors, what did it say about me? Above the sink, on the other wall, there were also many mirrors. It made me wonder how persecuted I feel, as if I have lost my sense of reality.*

There were many associations in that session, including to a friend of her mother's who had had breast cancer and a mastectomy. Emma remembered the name of an autoimmune disease that implies cell death.

At that session, Emma's intense anxiety was again palpable in the room, and I said:

> "Perhaps the many mirrors present in the dream refer to the question of how many mirrors one actually needs in order to see what has been happening, that can lead to cell death …?"

I also had in mind at that moment the many times Emma had looked at her vagina in the mirror, trying to identify what was happening to it. The looking in the mirror at her hidden, feminine sex seemed to be a way of working out the castration of her sex. How many mirrors does she have to look at to come to terms with her castration? These were my thoughts, which linked Emma's experience of being ill to her femininity, but I did not say so to her at that moment.

One is reminded of Freud looking at Irma's throat. Jacques Lacan described Freud's action of looking inside the throat of Irma in the following way:

> There's a horrendous discovery here, that of the flesh one never sees, the foundation of things, the other side of the head, of the face, the secretory glands par excellence, the flesh from which everything exudes, at the very heart of the mystery, the flesh in as much as it is suffering, is formless, in as much as its form in itself is something which provokes anxiety.
>
> (Lacan, 1978, p. 154)

The various phases of Emma's analysis were like these mirrors that reflected each other, like a fractal. In Phase 1, Emma repeated her anxiety in the face of the mother who had died, and her attempts to reach someone to help her. In Phase 2, chronologically later in the analysis but referring to earlier experiences and phantasies in her life, there was a breakdown into the somatic. Patient and analyst were facing incomprehensible, despairing attempts to reach an Other who is not there, indifferent, cruel even—a mirror image of Phase 1, but in the language of a regressive pull: there was no narrative, but acts and sensations being repeated over and over. This second phase can be described as one of pure trauma, with no content, expressed as a fear of a breakdown that has already occurred. At the beginning of the third phase, the conscious fantasies came to the fore. They now had a more explicit sexual content and an explicit sexual longing for the analyst. It reminds me of what Godfrind has called good secondary feminine homosexuality (2001), which is essential in the structuring of femininity. The erotic rapprochement with the mother/analyst and the identification it enables opens the way to the blossoming of a feminine sexuality.

On reflecting on the terms *Nachträglichkeit* and *après-coup*, Chervet (2009) has pointed to the masochism present in the word *tragen*, which suggests "to bear" and "to carry". *Coup* thus refers to sadomasochism, but equally to the traumatic. *Après-coup* points to the essentially traumatic dimension of a psychoanalytic treatment as well as to what enables that to be worked through. Its economic function is to transform repetition compulsion into the pleasure principle.

Conclusion

Analytic experience shows that there is a melancholic core to be found in the analysis of women, which is an expression of the loss of the maternal object that can never be completely mourned (Chabert, 2003). This melancholic core emerges in the narrative of the analysis and becomes a construction in the *après-coup* of the analysis. This melancholia can take refuge, however, in anxiety that floods into the room, or it can lead to a somatic breakdown, as in Emma's analysis, when we were thrown into a universe of bizarre bodily experiences that express both the longing towards that primary maternal object and attempts to separate from it: love and the hate towards the primary object come to the fore in a potentially lethal battle.

One can identify the different scenes in Emma's analysis. The first register was directed towards external events in her life. The second register involved a collapse into bodily and sensorial registrations, dominated by unacceptable affects that, until then, had not been thought about. It was experienced as a breakdown into the somatic, before symbolization could take place in the third phase, in a process of *après-coup*.

Many women's struggle to turn away and separate from their mothers involves a bodily symptom. I have often understood the bodily experiences of the women seen in clinical practice as representing attempts to have a body and a sense of self that is separate from the mother. At the same time, these symptoms seem to represent an aspect of the relationship with the mother that has not been properly internalized. This chapter proposes that a breakdown into the somatic points to the following: a melancholic core in the relationship with the mother; an internal, potentially lethal battle in the relationship between desire and renunciation that has not been elaborated. If this analysis illustrates that this somatic breakdown can reach such profound depths, it is my experience that the presence of transient symptoms is not uncommon in the analyses of women by women analysts. In such analyses the presence of somatic sensations and disturbances expresses primitive experiences of fusion with the ambivalently loved mother's body.

For Emma, the father did not offer an alternative to the relationship to the mother. As in the configuration present in the analyses of the famous hysterics, the father appeared, at best, as absent, leaving Emma at the mercy of the frightening maternal imago.

As a final comment, one cannot overemphasize the demands that such analyses place on both patient and analyst—the pain, the despair, and the collapse of symbolic representation—raising the analyst's anxiety about the patient's capacity to literally survive the process and transform it all into language. The process I have described is that of a massive regression to the somatic that expresses a refusal to separate from the body of the mother and the analyst. This process may take a long time to be worked through.

One is referring to something that had never before been put into words. Pontalis (1977) has evoked the experience of another space: words come from that space, and that it is not language that makes language.

From that space comes a narrative of death, sexuality, and love.

Notes

1 "We know less about the sexual life of little girls than about that of boys. But we need not feel ashamed of this distinction; after all, the sexual life of adult women is a 'dark continent' for psychology" (Freud, 1920a, p. 212). If in *The Three Essays* (1905d) Freud had postulated an analogous development in the sexual life of both boys and girls, progressively he was to discover the prolonged attachment of little girls to their mothers.

2 Kristeva's ideas evoke Leclaire's (1980) and Kohon's (1984) writings on the hysteric's main question: "Am I a man or a woman?" Kristeva argues for women's inherent bisexuality.

5

THE RIDDLE OF ANXIETY

Between the familiar and the unfamiliar

> The problem of anxiety is a nodal point at which the most various and important questions converge, a riddle whose solution would be bound to throw a flood of light on our whole mental existence.
>
> (Freud, 1916–17, p. 393)

In *Promise at Dawn* (1962), Romain Gary writes:

> In your mother's love, life makes you a promise that it will never keep. You have known something that you will never know again. You will go hungry to the end of your days. … After that first encounter, so early in the dawn, each time a woman takes you in her arms and presses you to her heart and murmurs sweet words into your ear, you will always do your best to forget and to believe, but you will always know better. You will always crawl back to your mother's grave and howl like a lost dog. Never again, never again, never again. … Wherever you go, you carry within you the burden of comparisons, and you spend your days waiting for something you have already had and will never have again.
>
> (Gary, 1962, pp. 24–25, in Hirsch, 2018, pp. 173–174)

Dimensions of anxiety

It is difficult to say what anxiety is, Freud tells us in Chapter VIII of *Inhibitions, Symptoms and Anxiety* (1926d). It is an affective state that is accompanied by physical sensations and bodily symptoms: heart palpitations, breathlessness, sweating, at times dizziness.

In Freud's first theory, anxiety is the outcome of failed discharge of libido. It refers to an excessive amount of excitation that is transformed into anxiety. Anxiety is overwhelming for the mind and is discharged into bodily symptoms. Strachey gives us the many examples of this view throughout Freud's work, from his letters to Fliess to a late footnote added in 1920 to the *Three Essays* (1905d). "It is a question of a physical accumulation of excitation—that is an accumulation of physical sexual tension. The accumulation is the consequence of discharge being prevented" (Freud, 1950 [1892–1899], p. 191).[1]

This perspective belongs to a theory of drives that examines the interplay between what is symbolized and what remains as an excess, not reducible to the field of representations but expressed in a symptom.

However, even during this period of his work, when he was developing the topographical model of the mind, Freud included reflections on the relationship between repression of phantasy and anxiety:

> Since the outbreak of anxiety is linked to these repressed phantasies, we must conclude that the *transformation* of libido into anxiety does not occur through defence between the ego and the *Ucs.*, but in the *Ucs.* itself.
>
> (Draft N, 1950 [1892–1899], p. 257; italics added)[2]

The second theory of anxiety was outlined more fully in 1926, although Strachey traces its origins as far back as the "Project" (1950 [1895]). Freud emphasizes the notion of a signal that is a response by the ego threatened with an experience of danger. It is a reaction to a traumatic situation. There is a sense of expectation (1926d, p. 165); a psychic element is now brought more clearly into play. Anxiety emerges as a marker of the uniquely human relation to temporality—one that departs from evolutionary time and is marked by a complex structure that moves between the present and the past, between *here and now* and *there and then*, with the predominance, in the last instance, of an *après-coup* (Perelberg, 2006, 2007). The signal refers to a danger already experienced in the past (the catastrophe that has already happened, in Winnicott's phrase) and which is about to happen again under the register of the compulsion to repeat.

Freud also distinguishes between anxiety and fear. Fear relates to an object, whereas anxiety has no object, although there is a preparedness for anxiety, in Heidegger's (1953) terms.[3] It expresses a distressed anticipation with no object.

The individual feels anxious but does not know why. Shepherdson suggests that the second theory of anxiety opened the way to different theoretical paths in psychoanalysis: on the one hand, the literature on the ego and the mechanisms of defence; on the other, concern with the subject and its ways of relating to the Other (2001, p. xxv).

Klein brought an important contribution in establishing a link between anxiety and guilt related to the destructive drives. In "A Contribution to the Psychogenesis of Manic-Depressive States" (1935), she proposed the distinction between two main forms of anxiety—persecutory and depressive—although the distinction between these two forms is not clear-cut. Persecutory anxiety relates predominantly to the annihilation of the ego; depressive anxiety is predominantly related to the harm done to internal and external loved objects by the subject's destructive impulses. Depressive anxiety is closely bound up with guilt and with the tendency to make reparation. It is the synthesis between destructive impulses and feelings of love towards one object.

Here, I suggest that anxiety is inserted into a network of other concepts that constitute points of reference in a structure:

1. It refers to *temporality*. The signal brings together past, present, and future; it evokes a sense of anticipation that something is about to occur (Shepherdson, 2001, p. xxxv), that "has still to be discovered" (Freud, 1926d, p. 165). Anxiety is "on the one hand an expectation of trauma, and on the other a repetition of it in a mitigated form" (p. 166). It is a "recognized, remembered, expected situation of helplessness" (p. 166). This is a uniquely human relationship to time whereby the following dimensions are brought together: repetition compulsion, the return of the repressed, fixation, repression, regression, the timeless of the unconscious, all under the dominance in the present of *après-coup* that will eventually give meaning to everything else (Perelberg, 2006).[4]
2. The idea that anxiety has no object establishes a link to psychoanalytic and philosophical theories on the negative. Anxiety thus

represents the encounter with *negativity*, nothingness and the void (Shepherdson, 2001, pp. xxviii–xxix). Anxiety has a "quality of *indefiniteness and lack of object*" (Freud, 1926d, p. 165). These ideas are also present in Heidegger (1953), who points out that "anxiety is characterized by the fact that what threatens is nowhere". However, nowhere does not mean pure negativity: "Nowhere, however, does not signify nothing" (p. 186).[5]

3. Freud has suggested that *Hilflosigkeit—the state of helplessness of the newborn infant*—is the prototype of the traumatic situation and at the origin of the experience of anxiety. The analytic situation is, by definition, traumatic, because it evokes the state of helplessness of the newborn infant (*Hilflosigkeit*), which is the prototype of the traumatic situation and at the origin of the experience of anxiety. Through the patient being invited to lie on the couch and say whatever comes to mind, within a setting where the rules are determined by the analyst, the relationship with the primordial object is brought forth. Within the analytic space, different dimensions of time unfold, and a tension between the old and the new is set in motion.
4. Following Klein, I believe in the intrinsic link between *anxiety* and *aggression* that is derived from the individual's destructive phantasies towards both self and other. Paranoid and depressive anxiety may be found in the same individual.
5. Anxiety also refers to the potential confluence between the *overwhelming presence—and absence—of the Other*. It marks the passage when the individual is still captivated by the other's desire, as in the quotation from Romain Gary (1962), or Freud's *Totem and Taboo* (1912–13), the world of the narcissistic father or mother, in which the individual is alienated from his own subjective temporality. The fear is that of disappearing in the enjoyment of the Other (Verhaeghe, 2001). The beginnings of one's subjectivity are yet to be achieved. One may refer here to the distinction between murdered father and dead father configurations (Perelberg, 2009b).
6. Anxiety is ultimately related to *loss*. Freud states that internal dangers change with the life cycle (1926d, pp. 146–147), but the common characteristic is that they involve separation from, or loss of, a loved object, or a loss of its love: birth, loss of the mother as an object, loss of the penis, loss of the object's love, loss of the superego's love. *Castration* becomes the signifier of

a dialectic relationship in sexuality and the profound sense of incompleteness for both males and females. The fear of castration requires the renunciation of incestuous desires and marks the inauguration of culture.

7. These ideas have clinical implications: in an analysis, *the analyst in the transference* becomes the repository of wholeness, of phallic intactness, for which the analysand is forever searching in order to feel mended.
8. In terms of its impact on the *countertransference*, anxiety may be overwhelming both for the patient and for the analyst, who feels implicated and a participant of the process. Joseph (1978) has suggested that

> The more the patient is using primarily primitive mechanisms and defences against anxiety, the more the analyst is likely to feel that he is being involved and used by the patient unconsciously, and the more the analysis is a scene for action rather than understanding.
>
> (p. 224)

The experience is that of suspense that there is something unfolding that feels familiar and yet will surprise the analyst. Something unexpected and uncanny will take place in the process.

I now turn to the clinical material that gave rise to these thoughts. The narrative unfolded very slowly in the context of the transference and countertransference. I emphasize the function of waiting on the part of the analyst for the meaning of the patient's anxiety to slowly unfold. Perhaps this is part of any analysis: one only knows what led the patient to seek an analysis quite some way into the course of the process itself. I shall briefly contrast this account with two previously published accounts. These examples illustrate that at times overwhelming anxiety on the side of the patient requires minimal intervention on the part of the analyst.

Clinical vignette: "Khalish"

A tall, slim, dark man with longish hair, Khalish enters my consulting room filled with doubts. His fragile and dishevelled appearance strikes me. His body seems to be planted on top of long, slim legs that are restless and awkward while he is sitting facing me. He speaks about being assailed by doubts centred on the question of whether or not he should stay with Mary, his partner of five years. Mary is a German woman whom Khalish first met when she was spending a year in Brussels for her studies, some 10 years earlier. They spent the year together; he then went to see her in Germany when she went back. A year later she returned to Brussels, and they began to live together. He has never been too certain as to whether he wants to live with her, or even that he wanted her to move to London with him. Things had just happened that way. His mother had been very keen on her and had said to him that he needed to give it a try. His mother's desire had been fundamentally present in the sequence of these events. He does not know what he wants. Should he stay with her or separate?

He is also feeling unhappy at work, with a loss of enthusiasm and a certain paralysis concerning his numerous tasks and responsibilities.

He is also not sure whether he is going to stay in London, as he hates his job as a commercial lawyer and thinks that he should go back to Brussels, where his mother, three sisters, and younger brother live. In the course of this first session he tells me that he suffers from vertigo. This started some 15 years ago, when his parents split up. At the time, he was terrified that buildings around him were going to collapse, and he was frightened of going along the street alone; someone always had to be with him. I understood that his parents' separation had left him with the experience of the collapse of the structures that he felt had sustained his life. He made a link to the collapse of the Twin Towers.

Episodes of vertigo occurred at least once every week.

Thinking that Khalish's stay in London might be short-lived, I offered to see him once a week during this period of crisis and transition before his move.

We started with weekly sessions During a period of a few weeks, he managed to break his foot and had several other falls while engaging in sports, when he damaged his shoulders and knee. For a few weeks, he came to my consulting room on crutches—a visible display of his castration anxiety, I thought. He had had a crisis of vertigo, after one of our sessions, at the tube station, and this led to a fall, which is when he also hurt his shoulders. My own level of anxiety increased at the progressive fragmentation of his body, I wondered whether seeing him just once a week was sustainable.

Background

Khalish is the eldest of four children and the only boy in the family. His parents were born in Belgium but are both descendants of immigrants from North Africa. They separated when he was 15. The mother had always been an energetic woman, a teacher in a primary school. She was the dominant force in the family, although some fragility was also conveyed. At the time of coming to see me, Khalish helped her financially. The father was a moderately successful architect, who occupied a passive position in the family. He was distant from his children and seems not to have demonstrated any interest in them. The children were all very close to the mother and to each other. They had shared two bedrooms as they were growing up, so Khalish had slept in the same bedroom as his next sibling. From a certain point onwards, it appears, his father had had lovers, and the mother had eventually kicked him out of the house. Khalish thinks that, in a way, all the children had kicked him out of the house, as they had been completely on their mother's side.

His perception of his family was that, for several generations, there had not been a decent man, with stories of rape, violence, and sexual abuse on both sides. Khalish's own father had been violent towards his wife; the children had often felt petrified.

Khalish did well at school until his parents separated, when life for the family became more difficult. The father contributed very little financially, and the mother supported all of them. Progressively, the children also started to work and to contribute.

Khalish was a shy adolescent, but as time went by he could see that he was a success with girls. He had a series of relationships with girls, which tended to last for a while. Most of them were foreign girls visiting Brussels, so that eventually they left, to go back home. This was an important feature, I noticed, and a key marker of the transference at the outset. I, too, was going to be a foreign woman, and our relationship was going to be of short duration—although it lasted a bit longer than I expected.

Sessions

In one of the early sessions with Khalish, I had responded to one of his long ruminations about Mary by saying that "perhaps it was not about Mary". This became a phrase to which he returned several times during the time we worked together. He had been telling me how beautiful she was, and his experience that they had a good sexual relationship. However, "something was missing". This had led me to think about his castration anxiety—"something was missing" in a woman.

A couple of months after we started our work, Khalish decided that he wanted to end the relationship with Mary. This was a painful process; nevertheless, they separated, and Khalish rented a flat of his own. He said that it was the first time he had ever lived on his own.

This inaugurated a period of enormous promiscuity. The discourse was that the women around him seduced him, with no reference to age: an older woman from his work, then several younger women whom he would meet in bars and clubs. He then organized an app on his phone whereby he got in touch with several women a day and could have sexual relationships with a number of women over the same weekend. After such weekends, he felt extremely depressed and upset. I felt alarmed that we would not be able to contain him within the framework of our once-a-week session. As it was clear that his departure from London was not imminent, I suggested that we should increase to three sessions a week on the couch. I had in mind that this would probably be a future setting that he would be offered in Brussels. He agreed immediately.

For the first few months of his analysis on the couch, Khalish's intense activity with women increased. He would tell me about the various sexual encounters over a single weekend. They were all foreign women in London, and the transferential implications were interpreted to him. I had thoughts about a phallic search in this need to keep an erect penis at all times. I also thought about Don Juan's hysterical symptom as being a way of expressing both his fear and his hatred of women—of his analyst in the transference. He did not know what he was supposed to do in this analysis, lying on the couch. Did he have to multiply his encounters with women as a way of protecting himself against me? Or was it an expression of his experience of the repetition of his sessions? I interpreted this to him. Another aspect of these encounters was that the women seemed to choose him, as, he felt, his mother had chosen Mary for him. *In the transference, the process had somewhat repeated itself, as I was the one who had seduced him into coming three times a week and to lie on my couch.*

Then, in a Tuesday session a year into the analysis, he told me the following dream:

There was a terrifying nightmare; a man with a blue head—he was cruel and disgusting. He was aggressive, naked, old, slim, his face kept changing colour. He told me that he was hiding money in a box next to the toilet. I screamed at him: I told him that I am paying for my rent. I am at his flat.

Khalish could not relate to the dream, and he thought that he did not know what it meant. After a while he said that he felt that *he had lost his pleasure in life since his father had left*, and he had cut all links with him. They had all taken the mother's side, and she had always insisted on how disgusting he was.

A: You are linking this man in the nightmare to your father; perhaps this man is also expressing an aspect of yourself that feels disgusting, old, and cruel.

[I thought that this old man could also be me, in what felt a very disturbing aspect of the transference, but I did not say so at that moment.]

He was silent for the rest of the session.

On the *Wednesday*, he came back and said:

P: This question of a negative self-esteem, I think that it is connected to the choices one makes … I was thinking about the man in yesterday's dream … You said that it was an aspect of myself. …

[A long silence.]

P: There is something which I have never spoken about. These are episodes with my sister [whenever he referred to a sister, I knew that it was the sister next to him, three years younger than himself].

He spoke in a very hesitant manner, in a very soft voice, and very quickly …

P: The first episode took place when I was 10 years old; she was 6. We slept in the same bedroom. We used to play this game whereby I would kiss her. We would join our lips, and we would keep them this way the maximum amount of time, without breathing.

The second episode is a bit later. I would have been 13 or 14 years old, at a time when I did not yet have any sexual activity, it was before I had even kissed a girl.

We were camping with my parents. It was on the very day after I saw that film porno with my friend. In the evening, we were in the same tent with my sister; my parents were in another tent. I don't have a precise memory, but we were naked and we pressed our bodies against each other. We did not speak. This did not provoke desire or excitation. It provoked guilt. I took advantage of my position, as I was older than her. I have always been terrified that my sister would tell someone what happened. I think that her bulimia has connections with what happened between us. She is unstable, and I think always that it is to do with these episodes. I did not have to pay a price for this, like she did.

A: However, you don't think that you are a good person; you think of yourself as cruel and disgusting. … Maybe you have paid a price too. …

P: All this problem that my sister has, I think that it is connected with me. It did not happen more than two or three times. Then I realized that it was not on. I don't know what to do with this. Nowadays she is married and has two daughters. Maybe she will never leave her daughters with me. I am sure, however, that I would never do anything to them …

[I thought that in this session Khalish was in contact with feelings of guilt and also shame.]

In the *Thursday* session, he brought a dream:

P: *I went into the girls' toilet. It is cleaner, more pleasant. There is another man there: we do that in the office, the girls' toilet is cleaner. I have a pleasant conversation with this man, the conversation is funny, friendly, feminized. It is a conversation that resembles a political meeting, surrealist. We don't do anything bad. I look for music on my phone.*

I go out last. There is a security guard in front of the door. A man walks in front of a bus. I tell him to pay attention. I am tranquil.

P: I wonder about this man in the toilet. I have always found men disgusting.

A: The conversation you have with the man in the girls' toilet is funny, feminized …

P: Yes. … But I am more attracted by girls. They are more interesting to go out with, to talk to, do things together. Physically, also I am more attracted to them, interested in them.

A: Maybe you wanted to be more like them?

P: I would like to be different from men. One time out of 40 I go to the men's toilet—the other 39 times I go to the girls'.

A: Maybe the man you have in mind that you want to be different from is the man that we were talking about yesterday.

P: Disgusting, yes. … From a certain point of view amongst the men it is always unpleasant. The ladies' toilet is always more pleasant, it is big, usually it is the disabled toilet. On occasions I had thought of changing the signs, but I decided not to do it, as it is not the title that is the problem. It is because men are disgusting.

[I noticed the link between being a woman and being disabled—there is always something missing in women.]

He continued:

P: When I was small and a witness of the life between my parents, I always saw my father as the aggressor. My father was always a bit of a roué with the women. My mother was never interested in sex, because he was always unsatisfied. I have been raised in an environment where all the men are very violent. I have now started to speak again with my father, for the first time in my life [this has started since his work with me], but I am not sure that he is interested in me. … He is more interested in my sister …

A: He is more interested in the girls …

P: The relationship that he has with my younger sister is very ambiguous. They go to a restaurant, and he takes her hand … once she was in ill, in bed, and he took advantage of the situation to tell his own version of the story. This has created a reaction in the family. She was helpless, and he chose this moment to speak to her, to impose his vision. It was perverse. With me, I feel the physical rivalry.

[A silence, when I was thinking about his own relationship with his sister that he might feel parallels his father's experience of himself as perverse.]

P: I hope that my father's relationship with my sister does not contain the same secret that I have with her. My father was always charming with my sister, as he was with his other women. I hope, however, that we can have a relationship that is close without having another secret.

My mother has always said that he was not capable of being a father. Her own father was violent and an alcoholic. I have been told that after she was born, he left for another woman. My mother went to get him: she knocked on his door, but he did not answer. It is awful to hear these stories. I imagine the scene. Obviously, he did not wish to have children.

In the last few months I have been in contact with my father again, and he seems to have an interest in me. We were caught between two fires, the children. My mother continues to accuse him. She continues to tell us new things about him that we did not know. Each day we wait for her to tell us something else horrible. Can we really trust her? I feel that I am immensely cautious.

I feel very disturbed about this fight between them.

A: Maybe it feels safer than to think that the conversation here takes place in a female toilet. It is cleaner, feminized, less disgusting …

Somehow it makes me think about the film *Les Demoiselles de Rochefort*—the absolute ideal, no conflict of any kind.

A: A world where there are only women—or, even better, girls …

Comments

This was a crucial week in the analysis. The dream that Khalish brought to the session on Tuesday enabled him to explore aspects that he had not spoken about until then. The dream revealed to him and to me his experience of himself as terrifying, perverse, and disgusting. Khalish screams at this man that he is paying for his guilt feelings. This perverse, aggressive man of the dream relates to an aspect of himself, but also of his father—the rage at his father for abandoning him to what he experiences as a universe dominated by his mother. Khalish offers the poignant statement, "*He had lost his pleasure in life since his father left*". His longing for the father is also being expressed.

There is a security guard on the door, expressing his longing for a male/police figure that will help him to feel safe. The potential suicidality is present, in its negative form. The man in the dream is walking in front of a bus, yet he feels tranquil.

This dream paved the way for the revelations, at the following session, of the secret that he had carried throughout most of his life—the sexual exchanges with his much younger sister. Feelings of shame and guilt are expressed that had been captured in the dream of the previous session, giving another layer of meaning to the dream; the relationship of guilt with his own superego.

At the Thursday session, there is another revelation—he goes to women's toilets rather than men's. They are more pleasant. It is where he feels more at ease. The phantasy that the analysis is like this conversation in the girl's toilet is expressed. The close relationship between his father and his sister is also revealed. Does the wish to be a girl, like his sister, indicate a wish to have a closer relationship with his father? Is it a sacrifice of his masculinity, a way of assuaging his guilt feelings for his perverse activity? The men in the family have been violent and aggressive. The anxiety of taking on a masculine identification is linked to their violence and perversion. He feels caught between his mother and father, in the universe of their *jouissance*, alienated from his own desire. The ongoing vertigo makes sense in this context. This potentially displaces anxiety towards an experience of fear as he is consistently at risk of hurting himself, bodily.

Further sessions

Several weeks later, just before a holiday break, Khalish told me about a scene in a toilet that had taken place when he was an adolescent. He went into a toilet, and a man was there with a woman. The man told him: "We are all repressed homosexuals." This marked him very deeply.

A: Another secret?

At the end of the holiday, in a Tuesday session, Khalish tells me that he had spent the holidays thinking about what I had said. What did I mean when I said "another secret"? Was he homosexual? He had spent a great deal of his time/life wondering about what that man (and I) had said to him. Was he, Khalish, also, a homosexual?

He then came out with the following revelation:

I have felt a desire for transsexuals for two years. I give myself to this bulimia with women. I love the power of seduction. I have retained this term that you used before.

[I had once addressed his intense activity with different women as sexual bulimia, in a session when he was referring to his sister's bulimia].

He continued: I was reading through my notes of the sessions. I write these notes at the end of each session. ... I spent the holidays wondering if I have homosexual desires. In the beginning, it was very difficult; I spent the second part of the holidays with this woman from Portugal. (This is a woman he had met just a bit before the holiday break.)

We spoke every day. Then we spent three wonderful days, when we got to know each other. We left each other with a great deal of emotion and now cannot wait to see each other again.

[Silence.]

A: The three days is what is possible ...

[I was still feeling confused about what he had been saying to me. Two years is the time since he had started the analysis. Is it since then that he had had the conscious thoughts about transsexuals? Is it an effect of the transference? Or has it been yet another secret? There is a repetitive association in the dreams between me and men, since that first dream about the man with blue head in the toilet. He also writes his own (secret) notes after each session (like me); now there is the woman from Portugal he sees three times in a week, the three times a week that he comes to see me ... the transference is present everywhere.]

P: I spent the first part of the holidays wondering if I was homosexual.

There was another episode I remember: when I was adolescent, I spent the night at the house of a friend; we slept in the same bed, and when I woke up I was caressing his back. We have never spoken about this. I and another friend, at the ages of 15 and 16, we used to masturbate each other. ... So, I do have all these examples and memories that I have not shared with anyone before.

In the *Wednesday* session, he told me:

P: The session yesterday has provoked a lot of cerebral activity. I have been trying to think about the theme of homosexuality. Perhaps the form of love I look for resembles homosexuality, because what I look for is tenderness, a caress, the warmth, the physical proximity, and afterwards there is a distance that resembles the distance in relation to my mother.

A: A conundrum that it feels impossible to address. Are you allowed to have another woman who is not your mother?

P: Do I wish to prolong the proximity of that relationship? What produces this unhappiness in me? I think I look for the truth and wish to be honest with myself and with you. Am I looking to prolong the relationship with my mother?

But I have never felt desire for a homosexual. Even when I was 15 or 16. Never, until these recent episodes with transsexuals. If I watch pornographic videos, they are of heterosexual relations, men/women, sometimes women.

Nowadays when I look at an attractive woman in the street, I think that it is false; when I look at men, I think it is bizarre. So, I don't look at anyone.

Now for the last months I have only gone to bed with one woman. [He is referring to the woman in Portugal. I also think of my couch.] I hope that this will work, although again she is a foreigner. There is something of a pattern that I recognize. I have the certainty that it will be short-lived.

A: Like with your analyst, an impossible relationship that you also think will be short-lived.

P: Yes ... perhaps I am not yet ready for a relationship ...

The over-sexual activity prevented me from reflecting on what was troubling me; it was a way of masking things. I now have a unique opportunity to think about my life, the trajectory from infancy until now.

I also have the impression that this whole story of transsexuals would not have happened if I were in Brussels. Yet, the first time was in Brussels. Is it a hidden desire? In Brussels, I would have a more regulated life. I would have more of a framework. This kind of sexual drive did not appear in this way. However, with Mary [the previous partner] I was very unhappy. I never wanted to go home.

A: Perhaps it was important to come to London and speak to a foreign analyst, as this creates a distance. …

P: Yes, I am sure of that. Yet the experiences also have a sense of foreignness and familiarity at the same time. Maybe because we can speak in French—that is my language. When we are away from familiar surroundings, is it that the desire becomes more unbridled? The transsexual has this strange appearance, strange and yet familiar.

A: Uncanny.

P: Yes!

[Long silence.]

P: I remember the first time that I had a sexual relationship with a transsexual was at this bar in Brussels. Men go there, men who are attracted by transsexuals. I went there before, a few times, but this was the first time I went with one. I went to her/his room. It was one of these transsexuals who had an operation. He did not have a man's penis any more. This disappointed me.

The second episode was in this same bar. It was a woman transsexual, Brazilian; she took me to a big door next to the bar. I followed her, and we went to the second floor. There were many clothes. We kissed, we were both very drunk. I slept there. We used condoms, but she did not want to. She did not have erections, but she had breasts and a penis.

I had the impression that I had a great deal of sexual curiosity. It was pleasurable. I was excited sexually. We did not speak at all. It was 100% a sexual experience. She is known, it was not frightening. I was in this bar with a friend, but he did not say anything when we next met. He did not ask me anything.

After that day, I had three experiences in London. Twice I was with transsexual prostitutes. I found them via the Internet. The second time it was after work, at the same site. I went to her, and I slept there. This time I did not pay.

Last time it was in Colombia, and there was this episode with a transsexual prostitute. This one I told you about. Thus, once I was with a transsexual who had had an operation. The other five times they had their penises. With four of them the activity was fellatio. In Colombia, he sodomized me, and I did not feel pleasure. Twice more I had encounters in bars; they embraced me, but I did not wish to proceed. So, this adds up to seven times. This is not a small number. I am shocked about the episodes that involved prostitutes. It is abject. It is like I was possessed. Each time after an orgasm I felt horrible. I have never told anyone about this.

A: Another secret.

[Silence.]

P: It is puzzling. I am talking about men who have the appearance of women. This never happened before I separated from Mary. … I don't feel attracted by the body of a man. Is it a homosexual desire that is hidden?

At the Thursday session, he says that he is less anguished by what he had told me. Is it the fact of being able to tell me all about it?

This session is centred on his thoughts about his father.

P: For Christmas, my father gave me a book of letters that a man sent to his mistress over 30 years. His idea is that we will both read them and make annotations in the book. He will be the last to read and will see all my annotations. I think that his idea is interesting. It creates links. This writer had a secret, passionate relationship throughout his life, with a mistress who was much younger than he. This whole theme is relevant for the family.

A: To understand your father's passion. …

P: Yes! The fact that he chose this book is interesting. It is a book about a secret. My mother had always said, since we were children: "everything becomes known", we end up knowing everything. …

I was thinking about a friend I had when I was at school. Her mother was a teacher, and her father was a taxi driver. He was diagnosed with cancer and lived still for some six months. Just before dying, he told the family that he was homosexual. A week later he died. When my friend told me that, I thought of what my mother used to say: "Everything becomes known." I thought that he took his daughter hostage. It was not a gift that he gave her. I think of this book that our father gave me. I have six weeks to read it. It is his way of creating links between us. It is a good idea. He chose a book about a secret.

[Silence.]

P: It is a good idea.

A: Perhaps in order to discover the nature of your father's sexual life? At the same time, you feel that you don't want to know about it any longer.

[Silence.]

P: Maybe I can now listen to him in a different way, that is not my mother's way.

A: Maybe they are becoming more differentiated, less entangled, for you: it is less the image of the transsexual. …

[A long silence follows.]

A few weeks later, Khalish notices that it is a long time since he last had any symptoms of vertigo. For a few months, he has also not had an injury. "Maybe I am more stable on my feet", he comments.

The fragmentation of the body

When he first came to see me, Khalish was trapped in an obsessional world "to be or not to be with Mary/mother"—a universe in which there was no place for the father. This father was perceived as violent, perverse, cruel, and dangerous, as emerged in the dream with the blue-faced man. Transgenerational issues were present, centred on violent men in the two previous generations, which impeded the mobilization of aggressive feelings towards the father.

In this obsessional world, therefore, there was no sense of a third (Sodré, 1994). Sodré suggests a differentiation between two modes of obsessional thinking: in the first, the oedipal situation is avoided, and thoughts connected to it are forbidden; the second indicates a configuration on the threshold of the depressive position, whereby the oedipal situation is omnipresent and thoughts constantly engage in rivalrous battles with each other (1994, p. 380).

Khalish's obsessionality at the beginning of his analysis reflected the former more than the latter. One is reminded of the Rat Man and his inability to decide between the two ladies. The Rat Man had become frozen at the threshold of the oedipal configuration, unable to elaborate his feelings towards his father and to move away from his mother. Khalish consciously withheld some of his thoughts, as expressed in his secrecy about the sexual abuse of his sister as a child, or his inner questions about his potential homosexual identifications. Issues of shame and guilt were therefore present for him. However, the accidents that he had at the beginning of analysis, whereby he hurt his legs, knees, and shoulders, and the persistent experiences of vertigo that he had endured for the previous 15 years, expressed conflicts that had not yet reached representation. Retrospectively, one can understand that he was also presenting a body that could not be experienced as sexual but was made up of bits and pieces that ached and fractured themselves. These defences against anxiety needed to keep being repeated. Freud states that the

> symptom, being the true substitute for and derivative of the repressed impulse, carries on the role of the latter; it continually renews its demand for satisfaction and thus obliges the ego in its turn to give the signal of pleasure and put itself in a posture of defence.
>
> (1926d, p. 100)

Symptoms are created "In order to remove the ego from a situation of danger" (1926d, p. 144). In Khalish's narrative and in the analytic process, it is as if the symptoms were multiplying themselves in order to keep anxiety at bay.

I believe that the increasing acting-out behaviour in the context of his analysis were unconscious attempts to give form as well as meaning to something not previously understood. The heterogeneity of symptoms expressed the fragmentation of meaning and Khalish's profound alienation in relation to himself and his own desires. He was imprisoned in the world of his mother's desires for him, in a universe where there was no place for his father. This provoked overwhelming anxiety that was repeated and magnified in the context of his analysis. The analyst became this overwhelming figure, both masculine and feminine, as indicated in the figure of the transsexual. Paranoid anxieties were then expressed in the progressive fragmentation of the body in the first year of our work together. In a very concrete way, Khalish was displaying to me his anxiety about the loss of integrity of his self. Was this not an expression of his castration anxiety, the threat to the imaginary integrity of his body? One could retrospectively identify Khalish's impossible experience of being in the world as a child, caught up between mother and father's seduction and violence in a way that was not possible for him to decode. Sexuality is fundamentally disruptive—because it is polymorphous, perverse, and decentring, hence enigmatic and anxiety-provoking.

Alienating identifications: murdered father and dead father

Romain Gary's pact with his mother, similarly to what has emerged in Khalish's analysis, requires him to sustain a phallic identification and a pseudo-masculinity. He remains an object of narcissistic satisfaction of his mother and is required to deny the desire for the father. The father as lover of the mother (Braunschweig & Fain, 1975) is evacuated.

Many authors (Green, 1999; Kaës, 2009; Laplanche, 1987; Perelberg, 2016d) have shown that the erotic and narcissistic bond between mother and child requires a work of the negative—the mother needs to "go away" so that in her absence representations and phantasy life can be created.

Faimberg (2005b) has suggested that "acknowledging the child as a separate individual involves the parents in an active elaboration of their narcissism, in order to permit the child to work through a genuine Oedipal position" (p. 9). When this does not take place, the individual is trapped in what Faimberg calls an "alienated identification"—that is, "the split or alienated part of the ego is *identified with the narcissistic logic of the parents*" (p. 10, italics in original). In such situations, there is no space "for the child to develop his own identity, free from the alienating power of the parents' narcissism" (p. 11).

Lacan suggested that anxiety arises when "the lack fails to appear", "a lack that is the condition of the subject's emergence, a constitutive lack-in-being that characterizes human existence as such …" (Shepherdson, 2001, pp. xxxi–xxxii). Anxiety emerges at the point between desire and jouissance. Jouissance expresses the experience of being trapped in the other's desire. Desire inaugurates one's own temporality.

Romain Gary's passage cited at the beginning of this chapter may be understood as an illustration of Lacan's views that at the beginning there is the desire of the mother *that may be overwhelming for the child.* The mother appears before the *infant* as *das Ding. Das Ding is not the empirical mother but the one that is produced as the unavoidable effect of the structure.* In the context of this chapter, it is the combined object of mother and father, which has taken shape in the body of the transsexual. Anxiety is a signal that the Other is too close, and the order of symbolization (substitution and displacement) is at risk of disappearing.

I have suggested this in terms of the distinction between the murdered father and the dead father (Perelberg, 2009b). The biblical example is that of Abraham renouncing the sacrifice of his son, so that the chain of generations can be inaugurated: Abraham, Isaac, Jacob.[6]

Khalish certainly came to his analysis presenting a configuration of the murdered father, imprisoned in the temporal dimension of his mother's jouissance.

Perhaps towards the end of this short period of our work together there was an indication of the beginnings of the symbolic, dead father. Anxiety is thus the threshold that must be crossed on the path that distinguishes two different modes of relating to the Other.

Progressively in the analysis a kind of madness developed. In the intensity of the acting-out behaviour, the analyst was being engaged not only as a witness but also as a participant in that the transference was everywhere. The compulsive activity involved Brazilian and Latin American transsexuals (or transvestites) and, finally, the Portuguese woman. The analyst had become the feared object that indicated the overwhelming presence of the other that both needed to be avoided and from whom he could not escape. The intense and compulsive sexual activity took place after a phase in which Khalish kept injuring his body. It signified, therefore, his attempts to keep his body as a phallic object, a penis for ever erect. The transsexual appeared as a phallic object. In the first encounter, when the penis was absent, Khalish was disappointed, as he was seeking an object who would have everything. His activity reinforced feelings of shame and guilt which also contained an element of self-punishment for the forbidden desires, expressing the subjugation to the severe relationship with his superego. It was only towards the end of the sequence of the sessions reported, when there was a progressive diminishment of the acting-out behaviour, that Khalish started to address me directly in the emerging dialogue. All this activity took place in the framework of the analysis.[7]

Images and the uncanny

In the sequence of the dramatic sessions that followed, the transsexual emerged as the combined object of the primal scene.[8] In the process of associations, the transsexual represented the lack of separation between the body of the mother and that of the father. This image of the transsexual, as it emerged in the analysis, gave unexpected shape to the underlying anxieties. The way it appeared in the narrative created an uncertainty on my part. Did I know about this before? Could the sequence of interpretations and associations have allowed me to anticipate that this was about to take place? When Khalish stated that "for the last two years I have been attracted to transsexuals", my experience was that he was saying it as if I already knew it—and yet, he was saying this for the first time.

Was this the irruption of the uncanny? Lacan has again suggested that the text on "The 'Uncanny'" is key to the understanding of anxiety:

> [Freud] after providing an extensive and brilliant series of examples while maintaining in suspense a definition of the term, he ends up by saying with Schelling, *that it is those things that, destined to remain hidden, have nevertheless become manifest.* It is what irrupts when it should not have appeared, what should be lacking is the uncanny. It is, moreover, *a sudden irruption that does not last.* It is an experience that, at a particular moment, comes down on the subject, *leaving him or her petrified and stunned.* It is anxiety.
>
> (Harari, 2001, p. 62)

The reference to family is included in the term *heimlich*, the family as the environment that gives rise to anxiety. Uncanny refers to that which is familiar and unfamiliar at the same time: the element of *surprise, disorientation that erupts*: "One does not know one's way about it" (Freud, 1919h, p. 221); "*Unheimlich* is the name for everything that ought to have remained … secret and hidden but has come to light (Schelling)" (Freud, 1919h, p. 224).[9] The word daemonic for the Hebrew and Arabic translation is the same word that Freud refers to in relation to the repetition compulsion.

Khalish's pull towards these transsexuals points to his castration anxiety; as with the fetishist, what is at play is the refusal to accept the lack of a penis in a woman. It is difficult to settle for an object that lacks a penis. It also expressed his longing for his father, his wish to be a girl, like his sister (or to say to the father: love me as you love my sister): "I wish to be my sister and yet to retain my penis."

When analysing the psychoanalytic literature on anxiety, Rosemary Davies pinpoints an apparent contradiction between separation anxiety (Kleinian approach) and castration anxiety (Freudian approach) (Davies, 2012). A potential solution to this is perhaps an understanding of castration as the signifier of the imaginary loss of integration to the self, which retranslates everything else *après-coup*. In the Freudian framework, the central function of castration as an organizer of difference means that retroactively it re-signifies all other forms of loss.

Despite many years of clinical practice, I cannot cease to be surprised by the unexpected that happens in an analysis, and the way in which *the analytic process gives actual shape* to something that had never before reached representation. These unexpected, uncanny, and dramatic moments generate experiences of anxiety in both patient and analyst. There is, indeed, a sense of disorientation, an inner questioning as to whether this was something that one already knew about, or had anticipated, although this new understanding only takes place retrospectively.

These images act like the mythogram of the individual's history. In Chapter 2 I indicated how a dream in which the patient Boris *was in a room surrounded by glass* led the analyst to visualize an incubator that became the representation of an aspect of his life until then unthought about (Perelberg, 2015; see also Birksted-Breen, 2012). A past that had not been registered at the representational level at the time that it had occurred had been repeated in the relationship to the analyst in the analysis. A narrative of a dream, together with the analyst's own experience of him in the consulting room, had led to a visual image that was then put into words, which led to some new information about his life. One was in the domain of the unthought known (Bollas, 1987). In Boris' case, the image came to the analyst's mind, although this was the outcome of years of tracking the elements in the transference and countertransference.

In Carolina's analysis, the patient herself had a hallucination of a wasp in one session that came to represent the experience of a dangerous and deadly maternal imago (Perelberg, 2016d). At the beginning of the analysis, the patient used to wake up in the middle of the night screaming, with no recollection of the content of her nightmare. We were, perhaps, more in the domain of the nameless dread.[10] With both these patients, these images (one produced by the analyst, the other by the patient) served as markers that led to a profound understanding of the nature of their transference to the analyst.

In Khalish's analysis, this took the shape of the transsexual. What all these experiences have in common is that they were the outcome of analytic work, phenomena that took place in the context of an analysis, indicating the work that had already taken place and that which was still to take place.

In the case of such patients, it is a failure of hallucinatory wish-fulfilment that is the basic model for an understanding of the psyche. This failure is the outcome of a traumatic encounter with the primary object. It is not possible to invest the mnemic trace, because of the pain or terror that it will provoke. Rather than evoking an experience of pleasure, it is an experience of distress that comes to the fore. Psychic reality is decathected; the patient withdraws into a "personal, bodily and sensory space of his own" (Urribarri, 2013, p. 293). Words are treated as things, as Freud suggested in his paper on the Unconscious. The patient is not present in her/his own discourse and in the session; he/she also feels like a prisoner.

In the treatment of non-neurotic patients, one is dealing not with an economy of unconscious desire, but with a "logic of despair" (Green, 1986a). This logic is less organized than that of the primary process and has to contend with unprocessed elements coming from the id. The aim of the analytic work is to transform symptoms and acting-out behaviour into words that create a narrative about the patient's history, transforming delirium into play and death into absence.

Notes

1 The intrinsic link between anxiety and bodily symptoms is very present from the outset. The first reference to anxiety in Freud's writings, out of the 255 references to anxiety in the body of his work, describes the symptoms developed by Anna O as follows: "A girl, watching beside a sick-bed in a torment of anxiety, fell into a twilight state and had a terrifying hallucination, while her right arm, which was hanging over the back of her chair, went to sleep; from this there developed a paresis of the same arm accompanied by contracture and anaesthesia. She tried to pray but could find no words; at length, she succeeded in

repeating a children's prayer in English. When subsequently a severe and highly complicated hysteria developed, she could only speak, write and understand English, while her native language remained unintelligible to her for eighteen months. Another example is that of Miss Lucy R: I will describe an instance which I happen to have analysed in the course of the last few days. I was treating a woman of thirty-eight, suffering from anxiety neurosis (agoraphobia, attacks of fear of death, etc.). Like so many such patients, she had a disinclination to admitting that she had acquired these troubles in her married life and would have liked to push them back into her early youth. Thus, she told me that she was seventeen when she had had a *first attack of dizziness*, with anxiety and feelings of faintness, in the street in her small native town, and that these attacks had recurred from time to time, till a few years ago they had given place to her present disorder. I suspected that these first attacks of dizziness, in which the anxiety faded more and more into the background, were hysterical, and I made up my mind to embark on an analysis of them. To begin with, she only knew that this first attack came over her while she was out shopping in the principal street" (Draft N, Freud, 1950 [1892–1899], p. 112; italics added).

2 Shepherdson (2001) has indicated that Freud's first theory of anxiety is more complex than usually understood in the literature. Freud states that anxiety in the first model is not understood as a purely physiological phenomenon, as it arises "by *transformation* out of the accumulated sexual tension" (Freud, 1950 [1892–1899], p. 191; italics in original).

3 Freud also distinguishes between *Realangst, automatische Angst,* and *Angstsignal.* The first is a response in the face of real danger. The other two, in contrast, indicate a disturbance in the psychic economy. *Automatische Angst* is the response to a traumatic situation whereby the ego feels threatened; it reflects an increase in the tension in the psychic apparatus. *Angstsignal* is the expression that something is about to occur.

4 It is reported by Jones that in a discussion before the Vienna Psychoanalytical Society in 1909, Freud stated that "every affect … is only a reminiscence of an event" (in Strachey, 1926, p. 84).

5 In 1927, Heidegger also established a distinction between anxiety and fear. Fear is always fear of something threatening, some particular thing in the world. Fear has an object. Anxiety has no reference to anything in particular, it is indeterminate. Anxiety is experienced in the face of something completely indefinite. It is, Heidegger insists, "nothing and nowhere". This leads Heidegger to link anxiety and the uncanny (Heidegger, 1953).

6 In *Des Noms-du-Père* [The names of the father] (2005), Lacan characterizes anxiety in terms of the knife held by Abraham and at the point of striking at Isaac's throat. When the angel descends to stay Abraham's hand, this is God's messenger, announcing the law that separates desire and *jouissance* and thereby transforming Abraham's relation to God, saying, in effect: "What God desires is that you should not use sacrifice as an attempt to satisfy His *jouissance.*" Anxiety is thus the threshold that must be crossed on the path that distinguishes two different modes of relating to the Other (p. 94).

7 Lacan (2004) has suggested that there is a distinction between acting out and "*passage a l'acte*": in the latter, the individual "falls out" of the chain of meaning. Lacan understands suicidal behaviour, for instance, in this way.

8 Klein has suggested the notion of the combined parent figure in several of her papers (e.g., 1929, 1930, 1932). In 1952, she described this figure as "the mother containing the father's penis or the whole father; the father containing the mother's breast or the whole mother; the parents fused inseparably in sexual intercourse" (1952, p. 79).

9 "[F]or this uncanny is in reality nothing new or alien, but something which is familiar and old established in the mind and which has become alienated from it only through the process of repression" (Freud, 1919h, p. 241).

10 "[A] state of meaningless fear that comes about in the context of an infant with a mother incapable of reverie" (Spillius, Milton, Garvey, Couve, & Steiner, 2011, p. 409). "It means that the patient feels surrounded not so much by real objects, things-in-themselves, but by bizarre objects that are real only in that they are the residue of thoughts and conceptions that have been stripped of their meaning and ejected" (Bion, 1962a, p. 99).

Part III

THE UNCANNY AND TIME

6

THE UNCANNY AND THE BEGINNINGS OF TIME IN *ONE HUNDRED YEARS OF SOLITUDE*

> When he was alone, José Arcadio Buendía consoled himself with the dream of the infinite rooms. He dreamed that he was getting out of bed, opening the door and going into an identical room with the same bed with a wrought-iron head, the same wicker chair and the same small picture of the Virgin of Help on the back wall. From that room he would go into another that was just the same, the door of which would open into another one just the same, and then into another exactly alike, and so on to infinity. He liked to go from room to room, as in a gallery of parallel mirrors, until Prudencio Aguilar would touch him on the shoulder. Then he would go back from room to room, walking in reverse. Going back over his trail, he would find Prudencio Aguilar in the room of reality. But one night, two weeks after they took him to his bed, Prudencio Aguilar touched his shoulder in an intermediate room and he stayed there forever, thinking that it was the room of reality.
>
> (Gabriel García Márquez, *Cien Años de Soledad* [One Hundred Years of Solitude], 1967, p. 143)

The mystery of one's origins and the differentiation between the sexes have been sources of wonderment for mankind since time immemorial. Myths, literature, philosophy, and art all explore answers to such questions about one's beginnings. Lévi-Strauss (1967) interpreted the myth of Oedipus as containing this fundamental question. The myth, according to Lévi-Strauss, attempts to mediate a conflict between a theory that attributes to the individual an autochthonous origin and the knowledge that any individual is born from the union between a man and a woman. The myth is an attempt to understand and elaborate the question of *how one can be born from two*.

One of the best-preserved figurative cave paintings in the world, in the Chauvet-Pont-d'Arc Cave in the Ardèche, depicts a partial "Venus" figure composed of a vulva attached to an incomplete pair of legs. Above the Venus, and in contact with it, is a bison head, which has led some to describe the composite drawing as a Minotaur (Thurman, 2008). Is this a depiction of the primal scene, of the difference between the sexes, or of the inherent bisexuality of humans? Freud believed that there are finite elements that can be symbolized: birth, death, the genitals, the maternal body, siblings, and the primal scene.

In "The 'Uncanny'", Freud (1919h) continued to explores these key mysteries. He sought the translation of the word "uncanny" in many languages: unfamiliar, familiar, strange, mysterious, sinister, disgusting, surprising, ghostly, frightening. In looking at the meaning of the term in other languages, is Freud attempting to master the foreignness of the uncanny? I am reminded of the various moments in his work when Freud appeals to a language other than the one in which he is writing. In the Dora case, he says that "*J'appelle un chat un chat*", when referring to Dora's genitals (1905e, p. 48); in his letter of 3 October 1897 to Fliess, when he refers to the episode when he saw his mother naked, he refers to her as "*matrem*" and her nakedness as "*nudam*"—the foreign language expressing, perhaps, an attempt to mitigate his incestuous desires (Freud, 1897). Is the search for the meaning of the word "uncanny" in a foreign language already evoking the anxiety connected to the phenomenon Freud is attempting to understand?

The uncanny refers to that which provokes anxiety and confuses temporality (past, present, and future), the internal and the external, the masculine and the feminine (Perelberg, 2016d, 2018b). It is to do with the prohibition to know what happens at night, when the children go to sleep. "Mama, who *is* the sandman who always drives us away from Papa?", asks Nathaniel. "There is no sandman, my dear child", his mother replies. All that I mean, she continues, "is that you are sleepy and cannot keep your eyes open, as though someone had sprinkled sand into them" (Hoffmann, 1817, pp. 86–87). The uncanny, as implied in this response, is that which the children are not allowed to know about. In Kurosawa's film *Sunshine through the Rain*, Kurosawa tries to depict through intriguing imagery one of his own dreams: a boy defies his mother's prohibition to see what happens between foxes in the forest when it rains. From behind a large tree, he witnesses the slow wedding procession of the *kitsune* (foxes). He is, however, spotted by the foxes and runs home. His mother meets him at the front door and says that an angry fox had come by the house, leaving behind a knife. The woman gives the knife to the boy and tells him that he is supposed to commit suicide. She warns that if he does not obtain their forgiveness, he must take his own life. Knowledge of the primal scene is punishable with death. Ignês Sodré has suggested the links between the uncanny, the primal scene, and death (Bornstein & Seulin, 2020).

Freud understands that the uncanny is the recurrence of the same thing. He explored *unheimlich* in relation to the maternal body:

> whenever a man dreams of a place or a country and says to himself, whilst he is still dreaming: "this place is familiar to me, I've been here before," we may interpret the place as being his mother's genitals or her body. In this case too, then, the *unheimlich* is what was once *heimisch*, familiar; the prefix "*un*" ["un"-] is the token of repression.
>
> (Freud, 1919h, p. 245)

Every individual has passed through his mother genitals. How to deal with this incestuous beginning? In *The Psychopathology of Everyday Life*, Freud suggests that what has to be included in the category of the uncanny is the fact that "what is looked for is never remembered".

> We must also include in the category of the miraculous and the "uncanny" the peculiar feeling we have, in certain moments and situations, of having had exactly the same experience before or of having once before been in the same place, though our efforts never succeed in clearly *remembering* the previous occasion that announces itself in this way. I am aware that I am merely

> following loose linguistic usage when I call what arises in a person at such moments a "feeling". What is no doubt in question is a *judgement*, and, more precisely, a perceptual *judgement*; but these cases have nevertheless a *character* quite of their own, and we must not leave out of account the fact that what is looked for is never remembered.
>
> (Freud, 1901b, p. 265; italics added)

One cannot, certainly, remember one's own birth, the experience of coming out of one's mother's body. The work of culture imposes a general repression and specifically the repression of that which Cabrol has called a *primordial incest*. The erotic maternal and primal seduction is at the foundation of psychic reality (Cabrol, 2011). Cabrol suggests that the birth trauma might be understood as a traumatic experience of a primordial mother–child incest that is rejected by culture and has also remained hidden from psychoanalytic theory. Might the analytic treatment, with its promise of rebirth and the prohibition of touching, re-actualize this primordial incestuous phantasy?

The uncanny is, ultimately, linked to the fear of the feminine and of the female genitals (Cixous, 1976). Jabe Marie Todd (1986) has argued that the text on the uncanny centres on the doll Olimpia, and that this is intrinsically linked to Nathaniel's fear of castration. The descriptions of Olimpia in Hoffmann's original text depict her as "heavenly beauty" (Hoffmann, 1817, p. 110), her "thinness", her "icy and cold" hands (p. 113), "wooden" (p. 116), with a "ghost-like appearance" (p. 115). Olimpia's robotic and frozen qualities evoke the contrary: the woman of flesh and blood, the father's sexual partner who may be fertilized (and thus has internal, live organs) and give birth.

Throughout his work, Freud makes many references to the uncanny. In the "Taboo of Virginity" (1918a), the female genitals evoke the fear of castration, one of the primal phantasies. Freud refers to the character of Judith in Hebbel's tragedy *Judith und Holofernes*. Her first husband was paralysed on the bridal night and never again dared to touch her. When an Assyrian general was besieging her city, she seduced him. After she lost her virginity to him, she beheaded him and liberated her people. Deflowering a woman involves the need to control the power of women plus the threat of castration.

In a previous paper I linked the uncanny to the question of what happens at night between a child's parents. There is an important reference to the sexual father:

I would like to point out, in addition, that Freud's exploration of the uncanny—"the perpetual recurrence of the same thing" (1919h, p. 234; 1920g, p. 22)—is centred on the story of the Sandman (Hoffmann, 1817). In the first part of this short story the main character, Nathaniel, recalls his childhood terror of the Sandman, who was said to steal the eyes of children who would not go to bed and feed them to his own children, who lived on the moon. Nathaniel came to believe that the Sandman was his father's mysterious nightly visitor, Coppelius, who came to conduct alchemical experiments.

One night, Nathaniel hides in his father's room to see the Sandman. Coppelius arrives, and Nathaniel sees him taking things out of the fire and hammering them into face-like shapes without eyes. When Nathaniel screams, Coppelius sees Nathaniel and flings him on the hearth. A year later, another night of experiments causes Nathaniel's father's death in the presence of Coppelius, who then vanishes without a trace. Nathaniel swears he will have revenge.

In this story, the Sandman is a representation of Nathaniel's aggressive feelings and phantasies towards his (night) father. These lie at the basis of the superego, which is derived from one's own aggressiveness towards authority, now reproduced in the relationship between ego and superego (Freud, 1930a). Both the paternal and the maternal are depicted in Freud's analysis of the uncanny. The "perpetual recurrence of the same thing" (Freud, 1919h, p. 234, 1920g, p. 22) is the stuff of any analysis.

Here, there is a marked contrast between Nathaniel's view of the "day" father, who is described as "mild and honest", and his image of the "night" father,[1] his features distorted into a repulsive and diabolical mask by some horrible, convulsive pain (Hoffmann, 1817, p. 91). The father at night can be understood as the sexual/diabolical father who then becomes like Coppelius—the counterpart of the mother of night of Braunschweig and Fain (1975). The concept of the censorship of the mother as lover (the mother of night) reinforces the impossibility of direct access to the maternal without the intervention of the Law of the Father. The demonic powers attributed to the Sandman/Coppelius/the night, sexual, father are derived from the repetition compulsion.[2]

(Perelberg, 2016d, p. 77)

Clara, indeed, writes to Nathaniel, her fiancé:

> all the ghastly and terrible things you spoke of took place only within you, and that the real outer world had little part in them. … The uncanny night-time activities with your father were no doubt nothing more than secret alchemical experiments they were making together.
>
> (Hoffmann, 1817, p. 95)

The text on "The 'Uncanny'", therefore, raises questions about the maternal and the paternal, the sexual of the feminine and the masculine, and the puzzle about the question of what happens at night between the parents. It provokes curiosity and refers to incestuous desires that are frightening, forbidden, and disgusting. Is it that the act of sex is, by definition, uncanny because of the experience that "one has, therefore, been there before"? Is incest at the core of the riddle of anxiety?

> [F]or this uncanny is in reality nothing new or alien, but something familiar and old-established in the mind and which has become alienated from it only through the process of repression.
>
> (Freud, 1919h, p. 241)

The uncanny is especially liable to arise "when the distinction between imagination and reality is effaced" (Freud, 1919h, p. 244). Literature is particularly available to create such experiences that imply "the experience of a suspended relation" (Derrida, 1994) between reality and fantasy. Everything is possible. One is navigating the realm of unconscious phantasies, of infantile sexuality, defined by transgression and incestuous desires, which are repressed, repudiated, experienced as the stranger in ourselves (Kristeva, 1991). The uncanny is thus profoundly liked to the object of psychoanalytic investigation, the unconscious, by definition familiar and unfamiliar, never fully knowable.

The experience of the familiar and unfamiliar evoke the notions of anticipation and retrospection, the two moments of time implied in the notion of *après-coup* (Faimberg, 2005a; Perelberg, 2006, 2007). Kohon has described the intrinsic links between the uncanny and temporality and the way in which the sense of uncanniness evoked by the objects of art and literature relates to a complex interaction between past, present, and trauma: "The past event is not endowed with a new meaning: the resignification is the reactivation of an already given meaning that was not registered in the first place …" (2016, p. 17)

I would like to explore these dimensions of the uncanny in a Latin American novel and in the clinical narrative of an analysis. Harold Bloom has suggested that what makes a great work of literature canonical is a sense of "strangeness, a mode of originality that either cannot be assimilated, or that so assimilates us that we cease to see it as strange" (Bloom, 1994, p. 3).

This sense of strangeness and wonder pervades one when reading *Cien Años de Soledad* [*One Hundred Years of Solitude*] (García Márquez, 1967), which deals with major and universal mysteries, such as a search for one's origins, incest, endogamy, separation, procreation, and death.[3] More specifically, there is a relationship between time and the formation of a couple that takes 100 years—a century that has allowed the author to write a novel that has become a myth of origins.

Time has not yet started in *One Hundred Years of Solitude*:

> Macondo was a village of twenty adobe houses, built on the bank of a river of clear water that ran along a bed of polished stones, which were white and enormous, like prehistoric eggs. The world was so recent that many things lacked names and in order to indicate them it was necessary to point. … [Macondo] was a truly happy village where no one was over thirty years of age and where no one had died.
>
> (1967, pp. 1, 9)

There follows a description of the introduction of secondary process, as opposed to primary process, and the timelessness of the unconscious. A visiting priest, appalled by the innocent but effective pagan system of "natural law", decides to stay and build a church. *Death introduces the beginnings of time.* The story relates the progressive inauguration of various institutions and the passage from magic to reason. Macondo becomes a "city with houses having mirror walls" (the appearance of the other).

Permutations in space and time

The narrative is situated in the past, even if it is still going to happen in the future (Jozef, 1974, 1980, 1986). Everything is known, however, because everything had been predicted by Melquíades, the gipsy, who wrote the history of the family "to the most trivial details, one hundred years ahead of time" (García Márquez, 1967, p. 421). The phrase "many years later ..." permeates the book, implying a freedom for the storyteller who knows the story he is telling and who may therefore stroll back and forth across narrative time.

Vargas Llosa (1971) has pointed out that the narrative moves in a circle, from undifferentiated chaos to political and social organization and back towards chaos. Frequently the narrative takes the reader to a point in the future and then back to events as they happen. The time of this novel is simultaneous, which means that while the events extend over 100 years, they also exist in one, shattered, time (Green, 2007). Melquíades does not place events in the order of man's conventional time but concentrates a century of daily episodes in such a way that they coexist in one instant. Thus, "it is impossible to establish distinctions between past, present and future" (Carlos Fuentes in Jozef, 1974, p. 62; see also Jozef, 1986, 2005).

The narrative begins with the foundation of Macondo and finishes with its extinction. The future in *One Hundred Years of Solitude* is always followed by a scene of return, of regression to the starting point; the same happens with the time that goes ahead, to the future. Facing this time, which moves in a continuous flow, there is a time that leaves an impression of eternity—it is what allows one to stay in the middle room of José Arcadio's dream. It is in this mythical time that José Arcadio is located when he says it is always March and always Monday (García Márquez, 1967, p. 355).

The interchangeability of past and present is replicated by that between life and death. Úrsula, at the end of the book, spends time in her room talking to dead people, and "no one knew for certain whether she was speaking about what she felt or what she remembered" (García Márquez, 1967, p. 347). It is this same interchangeability that allows Amaranta, as she is preparing to die, to offer to take letters to dead people. At the end of the book, Aureliano and Amaranta Úrsula are awakened at night by the traffic of the dead.

Ghosts levitate throughout the book. The ghost of José Arcadio Buendía remains for ever by the chestnut tree, where they had tied him when he lost his wits. Úrsula often goes there to talk to him, obeying a habit of her solitude. On one occasion, "she saw José Arcadio Buendía, soaking wet and sad in the rain and much older than when he had died" (p. 182). When the cinema is brought to Macondo, the inhabitants do not know the limits between reality and phantasy. The mayor proclaims that this is a machine of illusions that does not merit any emotional response. "It was an intricate stew of truths and mirages that convulsed the ghost of José Arcadio Buendía under the chestnut tree with impatience and made him wander all through the house even in broad daylight" (pp. 230–231). The different generations of the Buendía entertain many conversations with Melquíades long after he has died.

Repetition (and solitude and death)

The theme of repetition is central in the novel, which gives the narrative a sense of timelessness, in terms of the progressive construction of a myth of origins. It creates the uncanny experience that one has been there before.

Lévi Strauss has suggested that

> The function of repetition is to render the structure of the myth apparent. Thus, a myth exhibits a "slated" structure, which comes to the surface, so to speak, through the process of repetition. However, the slates are not absolutely identical. And since the purpose of the myth is to provide a logical model capable of overcoming a contradiction, a theoretically infinite number of slates will be generated, each slightly different from the others. Thus, a myth grows spirally until the intellectual impulse which has produced it is exhausted. Its growth is a continuous process, whereas its structure remains discontinuous.
>
> (Lévi-Strauss, 1968, p. 229)

But what gives myth an operational value is that it is timeless: "it explains the present and the past, as well as the future" (Lévi-Strauss, 1968, p. 209). This quest for *knowledge is, in the final analysis, a search for knowledge about one's origins.*

In the Oedipus myth, there is a concern with such a search, which proves to be disastrous, leading to incest, destruction, and death. This is also the outcome of Nathaniel's search, as he stays awake at night and hides to see the Sandman, with the catastrophic outcome that ends with the fire that kills his father. A major theme in *One Hundred Years of Solitude* is such a quest for knowledge—ultimately illustrated by the story that is written in manuscripts that cannot be deciphered. It is very interesting to note that the name Melquíades means "the son of the king" [*Melq* = king; "*íades*"= son, in Greek], hinting at what might be understood as a transformation of the Oedipus story.

The compulsion to repeat can be viewed as an unconscious effort to break through the repression barrier, in an attempt to break the rules of endogamy and of incest. The text that is finally deciphered by Aureliano provides him with knowledge of his origins, as well as of his destiny and of his death, at the very moment that he acquires this knowledge.

In the Buendía family, everything is repeated, and this undermines the inevitability of life and death. Doubles, as Freud suggests in his text, are an attempt to reach immortality. In *One Hundred Years of Solitude* the characters have the same names, act in the same ways, and have the same aspirations. In the names, everything is repeated: José Arcadio, Aureliano, Remedio, Amaranta, Úrsula. Even the signs of repetition repeat themselves. At the end of the novel the gypsies, who had arrived years—even centuries—before, return, bringing back the magic that had then produced astonishment and wonder. The differentiation between the generations is very frequently erased. This is what allows Santa Sofía de la Piedad to take care of the last Aureliano "as if he had come out of her womb, not knowing herself that she was his great-grandmother" (p. 364). The novel, in its repetition, provokes an uncanny feeling of anticipation of what is about to happen.

The narrative is structured around a series of narrative unities that appear to be circular. Vargas Llosa (1971) identifies 14 such sequences in the novel, each of which begins with an enigmatic statement about a future event. For example: "Úrsula had to make a great effort to fulfil her promise to die when it cleared" (-García Márquez, 1967, p. 339). The narrative then turns to the remote past, before coming back to the point when she actually dies: "They found her dead on the morning of Good Friday" (p. 349). This narrative is organized in terms of significant associations around events. The emphasis is on the imaginative construction, or what Vargas Llosa (1971) has designated "*episodios que muerden la cola*" (p. 545), which signifies the cyclical process of evolution and involution—birth, growth, decline, and death—and is also symbolic of a return to the beginnings.

The structure of the book is symmetrical. It has 20 chapters: the first 10 tell a story, the last 10 invert that story, as a mirror. The story itself is also duplicated in Melquíades' manuscripts. With the birth of José Arcadio's two sons, there is a bifurcation in the narrative. In each generation there are two antagonistic tendencies that confront each other (the Aurelianos were introverts but had lucid minds, the José Arcadios were impulsive and entrepreneurial), even if the positions are inverted in the third generation. In each generation one of the Buendías is shot and the other escapes, one has twins and the other does not, one dedicates himself to violence and the other suffers the consequences. The genealogy of the Buendía family is shown in Figure 1.

The dream quoted at the beginning of this chapter illustrates the whole structure of the novel. There are several examples of such repetitive sequences:

> [Amaranta's] life was spent in weaving her shroud. It might have been said that she wove during the day and unwove during the night, and not with any hope of defeating solitude in that way, but, quite the contrary, in order to nurture it.
>
> (García Márquez, 1967, p. 264)

The same circularity is present in Aureliano's making of golden fishes:

> Since he had decided not to sell any, he kept on making two fishes a day and when he finished twenty-five he would melt them down and start all over again.
>
> (p. 270)

This repetition marks the circularity of Macondo. In the succession of the generations, there are several attempts to enter the domain of historical changes: Aureliano attempts to do it through political revolution, José Arcadio Segundo attempts to build a canal to the ocean, Aureliano Triste brings the railway to Macondo.

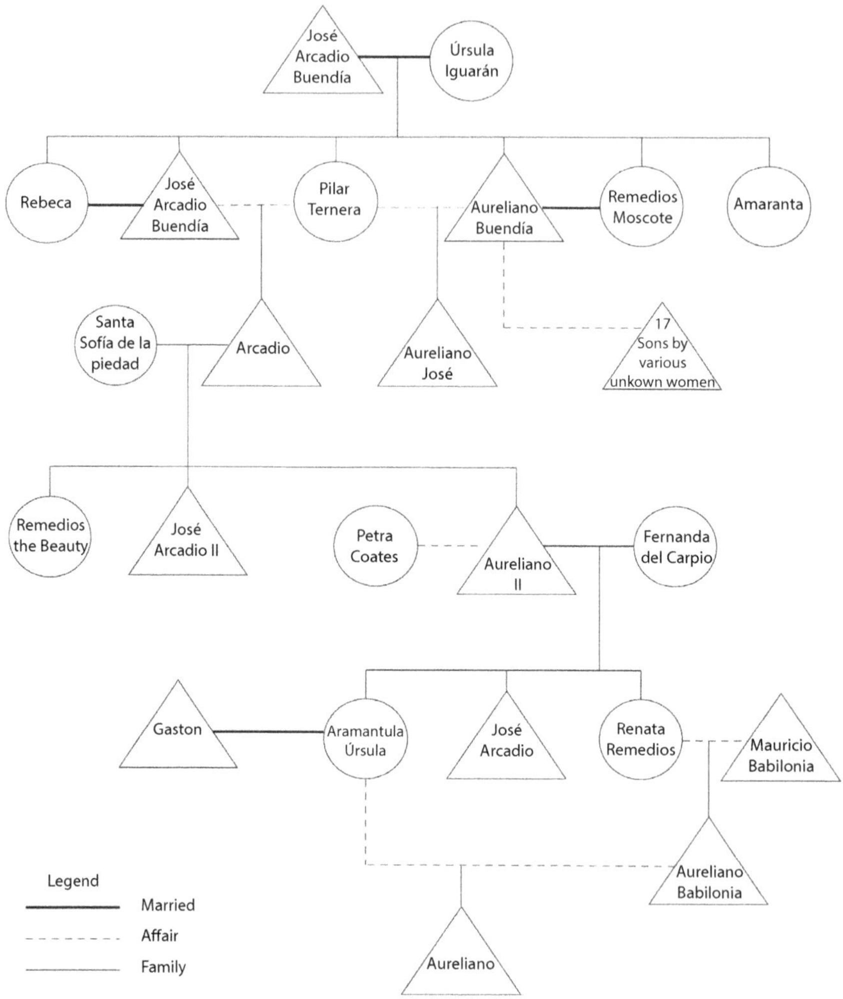

Figure 1 Genealogy of the Buendía family

Myth of origins

The novel can be viewed as constructing a myth of origins. This is a theme that permeates Freud's work, as he emphasizes mankind's concern with its origins and interprets the riddle of the Sphinx as being about where babies come from. This interpretation has been extended by several analysts (e.g., Róheim, 1946, 1950) who have suggested that the Sphinx refers to parental intercourse. The incest prohibition is characterized by Freud as perhaps the "most maiming wound ever inflicted … on the erotic life of man" (Freud, 1930a, p. 74).

The foundation of time in myths is, in so many cultures, related to intercourse between a couple. The anthropologist Edmund Leach (1961) suggested that the myth of Cronus indicates that the creation of time institutes the world of differences. In classical Greece, the sexual act itself provided the primary image of time.

In *One Hundred Years of Solitude* it is the whole world that is re-created, from its creation to its destruction, in a parody of the Adam and Eve myth. One starts with Genesis, in which José Arcadio and Úrsula, his wife, live together in a virginal way, marked by the shadow of an incest prohibition. Prudencio Aguilar's death and the couple's rebellion against the prohibition give rise to the Exodus and the curse that pursues the Buendías. They attempt to reach the "enchanted" place, a "paradise of dampness and silence, going back to before original sin" (García Márquez, 1967, p. 11). If the couple consummate their relationship, they will risk having a child with the tail of a pig. The book tells the history of six generations of Buendías where the relationship between the couple is problematic, not completely realized and thus denied.

Aureliano and Arcadio have a relationship with the same woman—Pilar Ternera—with whom each has a child. Arcadio, however, marries Santa Sofía de la Piedad, who is treated by everybody as a servant. Many years later *they had forgotten that she was their mother and later a grandmother in the household.* In that generation, Amaranta remains single, having a secret incestuous passion for her nephew. She is sensual but remains a virgin. In the next generation, Remedios and Arcadio remain single, and Aureliano Segundo marries Fernanda—cold, frigid, enclosed in her own world, a widow whose husband had not yet died and who spent her whole life as if it had been raining (p. 324). During the years when it rained, no one went into the streets any more. "If it had depended on Fernanda, they would never have done so … because she felt that doors had been invented to stay closed and that curiosity for what was going on in the street was a matter for harlots" (pp. 324–325). Thus, Aureliano Segundo has a passionate relationship with his lover, Petra Cotes, who, like Pilar Ternera in the previous generation, is the lover, symbol of sexuality and fertility.

Free and loved, she is also a prostitute, in contrast with the "legitimate" wife, Fernanda. In the next generation, Renata and José Arcadio remain single, and Remedios has a bastard son named Aureliano; he and Amaranta Úrsula, nephew and aunt, finally consummate the passionate and incestuous relationship that had been predicted generations earlier. It is only with this last couple that a "total relationship" is reached with a woman who, while being a wife, can also be a mother and a lover. This will then lead to death and the extinction of the Buendías.

The beginning of the book portrays a "screen memory": "Many years later, as he faced the firing squad, Colonel Aureliano Buendía was to remember that distant afternoon when his father took him to discover ice." He remembers the time that was prehistoric (with the prehistoric eggs), which was also a time when many things lacked names. Melquíades arrives, representing the part of himself that wanted to be able to see and know. Melquíades brings with him the telescope and the magnifying glass, and what Aureliano wanted to see is expressed in the following phrase: "In a short time, man will be able to see what is happening in any place in the world without leaving his own house." There is a prohibition on that wish to know (what is perhaps happening in his own house), expressed in the association between that screen memory and the firing squad that he is now, or "many years later", facing (firing squad = prohibition).

In *One Hundred Years of Solitude* the sin is incest, and the novel recounts the struggle that is created between endogamy and exogamy, knowledge and renunciation, incest and culture. The battle is present in each generation. *All these battles seem to centre around the question of the formation of a couple who can legitimately unite in sexual intercourse and produce children.* The last Aureliano was "the only one in a century who had been engendered with love". Knowledge and death come together, constituting a simultaneous process. At the end of the book, Aureliano searches in the parchments for the revelation of the instant of his own conception (p. 333), and this end *brings the book back to its beginning. Knowledge becomes associated with death.* When Aureliano Segundo meets Melquíades, many years after he has died, Melquíades refuses to translate his mysterious manuscripts. "'No one must know their meaning until he has reached one hundred years of age'" (p. 190).

The dream of the empty rooms is intimately linked to solitude—a word repeated 50 times throughout the narrative. The images emphasize the characters' solitude, and they end up isolated in empty spaces, like the empty rooms of José Arcadio's dream. They feel solitude in the empty rooms, which can be understood as the rooms where the parents cannot be found together and thus the knowledge of parental intercourse is avoided. The intermediate room represents that position of psychic retreat where this reality can be denied. In the circularity of the repetitions the recognition of a three-dimensional order is avoided, since the parallel mirrors can only reflect each other.

Enclosure is thus a defence against the experience of externality and a struggle against the experience of separation. When José Arcadio confuses his lover with his mother, Úrsula, he has reached and is experiencing both a new and an ancient state of being. "He is performing a primal act, something that for a long time he had wanted to do, that is accompanied by fear and a bewildered anxiety, and has awakened for him that fearful solitude." García Marquez describes Arcadio's ensuing nightly pilgrimages and sexual union as following "her path every night through the labyrinth of the room". Infected with a "virulent rancour against the world", which is a hatred of disharmony, he continues to long for the comfort of the woman who has defined, by opposition to her womb-like control, that sense of primal separation from one's mother. "We are fighting this war", Aureliano José is told, "so that a person can marry his own mother" (p. 127).

In the following generation, José Arcadio Segundo dreams that he is going

> into an empty house with white walls and that he was upset by the burden of being the first human being to enter it. In the dream he remembered that he had dreamed the same thing the night before and on many nights over the past years and he knew that the image would be erased from his memory when he awakened because that recurrent dream had the quality of not being remembered except within the dream itself.
>
> (p. 271)

The empty house with the white walls becomes symbolic of the relationship with the idealized mother-breast and of the phantasy of an incestuous relationship: what Chasseguet-Smirgel (1976) designates as the archaic Oedipus complex. It belongs to the archaic period in the individual's history, barred from consciousness with the repression barrier: the dream that cannot be remembered except in the dream itself.

Cien Años de Soledad constitutes both a myth and a longing for a return to a primary relationship. Freud suggested that a passionate sexual union constitutes a re-finding of the primary object. The end of the novel contains the passion of an incestuous relationship that brings with it the beginnings of time and also its end. While reading this novel, many times over, and many years later, I am still filled with a sense of wonder, surprise, and laughter.[4] Todorov (1970) has suggested that the uncanny offers an experience of limits, which characterizes Edgar Allan Poe's work, as well as Dostoevsky's (in Royle, 2003, p. 18) and, I would suggest, García Marquez's.

The quest for an understanding of one's origins and the nature of the relationship between the parents in the primal scene is at the core of our patients search in their analyses.

García Márquez once said that the ideal novel should "perturb not only because of its political and social content, but also because of its power of penetrating reality—and, better yet, because of its capacity to turn reality upside down so we can see the other side of it". Or from multiple angles. Perhaps this is also the stuff of an analysis that consistently presents us with uncanny experiences that take us back to the beginnings of time in the here and now, and the expression of a phantasy—very frequently strange and terrifying—that has never existed before.

Notes

1 The contrast between the "day" father and the "night" father is mine.
2 For additional interpretations of this text, see, e.g., Cixous (1976) and Todd (1986).
3 Most of the ideas described here in relation to *One Hundred Years of Solitude* were originally presented in the paper written with Bella Jozef (Perelberg & Jozef, 2008).
4 Royle suggests that "the uncanny is never far from something comic" (Royle, 2003, p. 2).

References

Abraham, N., & Torok, M. (1994). *The Shell and the Kernel*. Chicago, IL: University of Chicago Press.

Balint, E. (1973). Technical problems found in the analysis of women by a woman analyst. *International Journal of Psychoanalysis*, *54*: 195–201.

Balint, E. (1997). The analysis of women by a woman analyst: What does a woman want? In: J. Raphael-Leff, & R. J. Perelberg (Eds.), *Female Experience: Four Generations of Women on Work with Women* (pp. 36–45). London: Anna Freud Centre, 2008.

Balint, M. (1968). *The Basic Fault: Therapeutic Aspects of Regression*. London: Tavistock.

Bataille, G. (1957). *Erotism: Death and Sensuality*, trans. M. Dalwood. San Francisco, CA: City Lights Books, 1986.

Bataille, G. (1998). *Inner Experience*, trans. L. A. Boldt. Albany, NY: State University of New York Press.

Bateson, G. (1936). *Naven*. Redwood City, CA: Stanford University Press, 1958.

Benjamin, J. (1998). *Shadow of the Other: Intersubjectivity and Gender in Psychoanalysis*. New York: Routledge.

Bion, W. R. (1957). Differentiation of the psychotic from the non-psychotic personalities. In: *Second Thoughts* (pp. 43–64). London: Heinemann, 1967; reprinted London: Karnac, 1984.

Bion, W. R. (1958). On hallucination. *International Journal of Psychoanalysis*, *39*: 341–349. In: *Second Thoughts* (pp. 65–85). London: Heinemann, 1967; reprinted London: Karnac, 1984.

Bion, W. R. (1959). Attacks on linking. In: *Second Thoughts* (pp. 93–109). London: Heinemann, 1967; reprinted London: Karnac, 1984.

Bion, W. R. (1962a). *Learning from Experience*. London: Heinemann.

Bion, W. R. (1962b). A theory of thinking. In: *Second Thoughts* (pp. 110–119). London: Heinemann, 1967; reprinted London: Karnac,

1984. [First published as: The psycho-analytic study of thinking. *International Journal of Psychoanalysis, 43*: 306–310.]

Bion, W. R. (1965). *Transformations*. London: Heinemann, reprinted London: Karnac, 1984.

Bion, W. R. (1970). *Attention and Interpretation*. London: Tavistock Publications.

Bion, W. R. (1992). *Cogitations*. London: Karnac.

Birksted-Breen, D. (1989). Working with an anorexic patient. *International Journal of Psychoanalysis, 70*: 29–40. Also in: J. Raphael-Leff & R. J. Perelberg (Eds.), *Female Experience: Four Generations of Women on Work with Women* (pp. 104–122). London: Anna Freud Centre, 2008.

Birksted-Breen, D. (2009). "Reverberation time", dreaming and the capacity to dream. *International Journal of Psychoanalysis, 90*: 35–51.

Birksted-Breen, D. (2012). Taking time: The tempo of psychoanalysis. *International Journal of Psychoanalysis, 93*: 819–835.

Bloom, H. (1994). *The Western Canon*. London: Macmillan.

Blum, H. P. (1971). On the conception and development of the transference neurosis. *Journal of the American Psychoanalytic Association, 19*: 41–53.

Bokanowski, T. (2010). Rêve, transferts et scène primitive chez l'Homme aux loups. *Revue Française de Psychanalyse, 4* (74): 969–980.

Bollas, C. (1987). *The Shadow of the Object: Psychoanalysis of the Unthought Known*. London: Free Association Books.

Boris, H. (1984). The problem of anorexia nervosa. *International Journal of Psychoanalysis, 65*: 315–322.

Bornstein, C., & Seulin, C. (2020). *The Uncanny Revisited*. London: Routledge, forthcoming.

Botella, C., & Botella, S. (2005). *Psychic Figurability*. London: Routledge.

Botella, C., & Botella, S. (2013). Psychic figurability and unrepresented states. In: H. B. Levine, D. Scarfone, & G. B. Reed (Eds.), *Unrepresented States and the Construction of Meaning* (pp. 95–121). London: Karnac.

Braunschweig, D., & Fain, M. (1975). *La nuit, le jour. Essai psychanalytique sur le fonctionnement mental [Night, Day: A Psychoanalytic Essay on Mental Functioning]*. Paris: Presses Universitaires de France.

Brierley, M. (1932). Some problems of integration in women. *International Journal of Psychoanalysis, 13*: 433–448.

Britton, R. (2003). Narcissistic problems in sharing space. In: *Sex, Death and the Superego* (pp. 164–178). London: Karnac.

Budd, S. (2005). The psychogenesis of a case of female homosexuality. In: R. J. Perelberg (Ed.), *Freud: A Modern Reader* (pp. 234–250). London: Wiley.

Burgner, M. (1997). Analytic treatment of an adolescent with bulimia nervosa. In: J. Raphael-Leff & R. J. Perelberg (Eds.), *Female Experience:*

Four Generations of Women on Work with Women (pp. 93–103). London: Anna Freud Centre, 2008.

Butler, J. (1990). *Gender Trouble: Feminism and the Subversion of Identity*. London: Routledge.

Butler, J. (1993). *Bodies that Matter: On the Discursive Limits of "Sex"*. London: Routledge.

Butler, J. (2015). Ideologies of the super-ego: Psychoanalysis and feminism revisited. In: T. Duschinsky & S. Walker (Eds.), *Juliet Mitchell and the Lateral Axis* (pp. 57–76). New York: Palgrave.

Cabrol, G. (2011). Le refoulement de l'inceste primordial. *Revue Française de Psychanalyse, 75* (December): 1583–1587.

Cadogan Hall Programme. (2014). *Pinchas Zukerman—Summer Music Festival with. "Enigma" Variations, Op. 36*. London: Cadogan Hall.

Campbell, D. (2018). Alienating identifications and sexuality. In: R. J. Perelberg (Ed.), *Psychic Bisexuality: A British–French Dialogue* (pp. 227–242). London: Routledge.

Chabert, C. (2003). *Féminin mélancolique [The Melancholic Feminine]*. Paris: Presses Universitaires de France.

Chabert, C. (2005). Clinical and metapsychological reflections on "A Child Is Being Beaten". In: R. J. Perelberg (Ed.), *Freud: A Modern Reader* (pp. 224–233). London: Wiley.

Chabert, C. (2018). Tell me whom you like best. In: R. J. Perelberg (Ed.), *Psychic Bisexuality: A British–French Dialogue* (pp. 81–89). London: Routledge.

Chasseguet-Smirgel, J. (1964). *Female Sexuality: New Psychoanalytic Views*. Ann Arbor, MI: University of Michigan Press, 1970; reprinted London: Karnac, 1991.

Chasseguet-Smirgel, J. (1976). Freud and female sexuality: The consideration of some blind spots in the exploration of the "dark continent". *International Journal of Psychoanalysis, 57*: 275–286.

Chasseguet-Smirgel, J. (1984). *Ethique et Esthétique de la Perversion*. Paris: Champ Vallon.

Chasseguet-Smirgel, J. (1986). *Sexuality and Mind*. New York: New York University Press.

Chemouni, J. (2013). *Pour Introduire le Narcissisme*. Paris: Editions in Press.

Chervet, B. (2009). L'après-coup. La tentative d'inscrire ce qui tend à disparaitre. *Revue Française de Psychanalyse, 73*: 1361–1442.

Chiland, C. (2005). *Exploring Transsexualism*, trans. D. Alcorn. London: Karnac.

Cixous, H. (1976). Fiction and its phantoms: A reading of Freud's "Das Unheimliche". *New Literary History*, 7: 525–548.

Cournut-Janin, M. (1998). *Féminin et féminité*. Paris: Presses Universitaires de France.

Cournut-Janin, M. (2005). Dora: Fragment of an analysis of hysteria. In: R. J. Perelberg (Ed.), *Freud: A Modern Reader* (pp. 47–60). London: Wiley.

Cournut-Janin, M., & Cournut, J. (1993). La castration et le féminin dans les deux sexes. *Revue Française de Psychanalyse, 5*: 1353–1558.

Davies, R. (2012). Anxiety: The importunate companion: Psychoanalytic theory of castration and separation anxiety and implications for clinical technique. *International Journal of Psychoanalysis, 93*: 1101–1114.

De Masi, F., Davalli, C., Giustino, G., & Pergami, A. (2015). Hallucinations in the psychotic state: Psychoanalysis and the neurosciences compared. *International Journal of Psychoanalysis, 96*: 293–318.

Derrida, J. (1994). *Spectres of Marx: The State of Debts, the Work of Mourning, and the New International*, trans. P. Kamuf. London: Routledge.

Dimen, M. (1991). Deconstructing difference: Gender, splitting and "transitional space". *Psychoanalytic Dialogue, 1*: 335–352.

Donnet, J. -L., & Green, A. (1973). *L'Enfant de Ça.* Paris: Editions de Minuit.

Dor, J. (1998). *Introduction to the Reading of Lacan.* New York: Other Press.

Faimberg, H. (2005a). Après-coup. *International Journal of Psychoanalysis, 86* (1): 1–6.

Faimberg, H. (2005b). *The Telescoping of Generations: Listening to the Narcissistic Links between Generations.* London: Karnac.

Fairbairn, W. R. D. (1931). Features in the analysis of a patient with a physical genital abnormality. In: *Psychoanalytic Studies of the Personality* (pp. 197–222). London: Routledge, 1994.

Fairbairn, W. R. D. (1940). Schizoid factors in the personality. In: *Psychoanalytic Studies of the Personality* (pp. 3–27). London: Routledge, 1994.

Faludi, S. (2017). *In the Dark Room.* London: William Collins.

Ferenczi, S. (1932). Confusion of tongues between adults and the child: The language of tenderness and of passion. In: *Final Contributions to the Problems and Methods of Psychoanalysis.* New York: Basic Books, 1955.

Ferro, N. (2002). Superego transformations through the analyst's capacity for reverie. *Psychoanalytic Quarterly, 71*: 477–501.

Freud, S. (1893). Case histories: Miss Lucy R. *Standard Edition, 2*: 106–124.

Freud, S. (1895b). On the grounds for detaching a particular syndrome from neurasthenia under the description "anxiety neurosis". *Standard Edition, 3*: 85–115.

Freud, S. (1895d) (with Breuer, J.). *Studies on Hysteria. Standard Edition, 2.*

Freud, S. (1897). Letter from Freud to Fliess, December 12, 1897. In: J. M. Masson (Ed.), *The Complete Letters of Sigmund Freud to Wilhelm Fliess, 1887–1904* (pp. 285–287). Cambridge, MA: Belknap Press.

Freud, S. (1900a). *The Interpretation of Dreams. Standard Edition,* 4–5.

Freud, S. (1901b). *The Psychopathology of Everyday Life. Standard Edition, 6.*

Freud, S. (1905d). *Three Essays on the Theory of Sexuality. Standard Edition, 7*: 123–245.

Freud, S. (1905e). Fragment of an analysis of a case of hysteria. *Standard Edition, 7*: 1–122.

Freud, S. (1907a). Delusions and dreams in Jensen's *Gradiva. Standard Edition, 9*: 1–96.

Freud, S. (1908a). Hysterical phantasies and their relation to bisexuality. *Standard Edition, 8*: 155–166.

Freud, S. (1909b). Analysis of a phobia in a five-year-old boy. *Standard Edition, 9*: 1–150.

Freud, S. (1909d). Notes upon a case of obsessional neurosis. *Standard Edition, 10*: 153–320.

Freud, S. (1911b). Formulations on the two principles of mental functioning. *Standard Edition, 12*: 213–226.

Freud, S. (1911c). Psycho-analytic notes on an autobiographical account of a case of paranoia. *Standard Edition, 12*: 3–82.

Freud, S. (1912–13). *Totem and Taboo. Standard Edition, 13*: 1–161.

Freud, S. (1914a). Fausse reconnaissance ("déjà raconté") in psycho-analytic treatment. *Standard Edition, 13*: 199–207.

Freud, S. (1914c). On narcissism: An introduction. *Standard Edition, 14*: 73–102.

Freud, S. (1914g). Remembering, repeating and working-through [Further recommendations on the technique of psycho-analysis]. *Standard Edition, 12*: 147–156.

Freud, S. (1915e). The unconscious. *Standard Edition, 14*: 159–209.

Freud, S. (1916–17). *Introductory Lectures on Psycho-Analysis. Standard Edition*, 15–16.

Freud, S. (1917d). A metapsychological supplement to the theory of dreams. *Standard Edition, 14*: 217–235.

Freud, S. (1917e). Mourning and melancholia. *Standard Edition, 14*: 237–258.

Freud, S. (1918a). The taboo of virginity. *Standard Edition, 11*: 193–208.

Freud, S. (1918b). From the history of an infantile neurosis. *Standard Edition, 17*: 3–123.

Freud, S. (1919e). "A child is being beaten": A contribution to the study of the genesis of sexual perversions. *Standard Edition, 17*: 195–204.

Freud, S. (1919h). The "uncanny". *Standard Edition, 17*: 217–256.

Freud, S. (1920a). The psychogenesis of a case of homosexuality in a woman. *Standard Edition, 18*: 147–172.

Freud, S. (1920g). *Beyond the Pleasure Principle. Standard Edition, 18*: 7–64.

Freud, S. (1923b). *The Ego and the Id. Standard Edition, 19*: 12–66.

Freud, S. (1924c). The economic problem of masochism. *Standard Edition, 19*: 159–170.

Freud, S. (1924d). The dissolution of the Oedipus complex. *Standard Edition, 19*: 173–179.

Freud, S. (1925h). Negation. *Standard Edition, 19*: 235–240.

Freud, S. (1926d). *Inhibitions, Symptoms and Anxiety. Standard Edition, 20*: 77–175.

Freud, S. (1930a). *Civilization and Its Discontents. Standard Edition, 21.*

Freud, S. (1931b). Female sexuality. *Standard Edition, 21*: 223–246.

Freud, S. (1933a). *New Introductory Lectures on Psycho-Analysis. Standard Edition, 22*: 3–182.

Freud, S. (1937c). Analysis terminable and interminable. *Standard Edition, 23*: 209–253.

Freud, S. (1937d). Constructions in analysis. *Standard Edition, 23*: 255–269.

Freud, S. (1940 [1938]). *An Outline of Psycho-Analysis. Standard Edition, 23*: 141–208.

Freud, S. (1950 [1892–1899]). Extracts from the Fliess Papers. *Standard Edition, 1*: 173–280.

Freud, S. (1950 [1895]). Project for a scientific psychology. *Standard Edition, 1*: 281.

García Márquez, G. (1967). *One Hundred Years of Solitude.* London: Penguin, 1970.

Gary, R. (1962). *Promise at Dawn,* trans. J. M. Beach. London: Michael Joseph. [*La promesse de l'aube.* Paris: Gallimard, 1960.]

Gherovici, P. (2010). *Please Select Your Gender: From the Invention of Hysteria to the Democratizing of Transgenderism.* New York: Routledge.

Glasser, M. (1979). Some aspects of the role of aggression in the perversions. In: I. Rosen (Ed.), *Sexual Deviation* (pp. 278–305). Oxford: Oxford University Press.

Glover, E. (1955). *The Technique of Psychoanalysis.* New York: International Universities Press.

Godfrind, J. (2001). *Comment la féminité vient aux femmes.* Paris: Presses Universitaires de France.

Gozlan, O. (2015). *Transsexuality and the Art of Transitioning: A Lacanian Approach.* London: Routledge.

Green, A. (1973). Le genre neutre. In: *Bisexualité et la différence des sexes.* Nouvelle Revue de Psychanalyse, No. 7. Paris: Gallimard. Also in: *Narcissisme de vie. Narcissism de mort* (pp. 208–221). Paris: Minuit, 1983. [The neuter gender. In: *Life Narcissism, Death Narcissism* (pp. 158–169), trans. A. Weller. London: Free Association Books, 2001. Also in: R. J. Perelberg (Ed.), *Psychic Bisexuality: A British–French Dialogue* (pp. 243–257). London: Routledge, 2018.]

Green, A. (1975). The analyst, symbolization and absence in the analytic setting (On changes in analytic practice and analytic experience)—In memory of D. W. Winnicott. *International Journal of Psychoanalysis, 56*: 1–22.

Green, A. (1983). The dead mother. In: *Life Narcissism, Death Narcissism* (pp. 170–200), trans. A. Weller. London: Free Association Books, 2001.

Green, A. (1986a). The borderline concept. In: *On Private Madness* (pp. 60–83). London: Hogarth Press & The Institute of Psychoanalysis.

Green, A. (1986b). The dead mother. In: *On Private Madness* (pp. 142–173). London: Hogarth Press & The Institute of Psychoanalysis.

Green, A. (1986c). Passions and their vicissitudes. In: *On Private Madness* (pp. 214–253). London: Hogarth Press & The Institute of Psychoanalysis.

Green, A. (1995). *Propédeutique. La métapsychologie revisitée.* Seyssel: Champ Vallon.

Green, A. (1998). The primordial mind and the work of the negative. *International Journal of Psychoanalysis, 79*: 649–665.

Green, A. (1999). *The Work of the Negative*, trans. A. Weller. London: Free Association Books.

Green, A. (2001). *Life Narcissism, Death Narcissism*, trans. A. Weller. London: Free Association Books.

Green, A. (2002a). *Idées directrices pour une psychanalyse contemporaine.* Paris: Presses Universitaires de France.

Green, A. (2002b). *Time in Psychoanalysis.* London: Free Associations Books.

Green, A. (2005a). L'Intuition du negatif dans "Jeu et realite". In: *Jouer avec Winnicott.* Paris: Presses Universitaires de France.

Green, A. (2005b). *Key Ideas for a Contemporary Psychoanalysis: Misrecognition and Recognition of the Unconscious*, trans. A. Weller. London: Routledge.

Green, A. (2005c). Negation. In: R. J. Perelberg (Ed.), *Freud: A Modern Reader* (pp. 253–274). London: Whurr.

Green, A. (2007). The construction of heterochrony. In: R. J. Perelberg (Ed.), *Time and Memory* (pp. 1–22). London: Karnac.

Grinberg, L. (1962). On a specific aspect of countertransference due to the patient's projective identification. *International Journal of Psychoanalysis, 43*: 436.

Harari, R. (2001). *Lacan's Seminar on Anxiety: An Introduction.* New York: Other Press.

Haraway, D. J. (1991). *Simians, Cyborgs and Women.* London: Free Association Books.

Harmann, P. (Ed.) (1958). Lettre de Rimbaud à Georges Izambard—13 mai 1871. In: *Œuvres* (pp. 305–306). Paris: Mercure de France (impr. Aulard).

Harris, A. (1991). Gender as contradiction. *Psychoanalytic Dialogues, 1* (2): 197–224.

Harris, A. (2005). *Gender as Soft Assembly*. Hillsdale, NJ: Analytic Press.

Heidegger, M. (1953). *Being and Time*. Albany, NY: State University of New York Press.

Heimann, P. (1950). On counter-transference. *International Journal of Psychoanalysis, 31*: 81–84.

Héritier, F. (2002). *Masculin/féminin, II. Dissoudre la hiérarchie*. Paris: Odile Jacob.

Héritier, F. (2012). *Masculin/féminin, I*. Paris: Odile Jacob.

Hirsch, D. (2018). Unconscious pacts and the bisexuality of the countertransference in the psychoanalytic process. In: R. J. Perelberg (Ed.), *Psychic Bisexuality: A British–French Dialogue* (pp. 170–188). London: Routledge.

Hoffmann, E. T. A. (1817). The Sandman. In: *Tales of Hoffmann*. London: Penguin, 1982.

Irigaray, L. (1989). The gesture in psychoanalysis. In: T. Brenman (Ed.), *Between Feminism and Psychoanalysis* (pp. 127–138). London: Routledge.

Isaacs, S. (1948). The nature and function of phantasy. *International Journal of Psychoanalysis, 29*: 73–97.

Jones, E. (1974). *Sigmund Freud: Life and Work*. London: Hogarth Press.

Joseph, B. (1978). Different types of anxiety and their handling in the analytic situation. *International Journal of Psychoanalysis, 59*: 223–228.

Joseph, B. (1985). Transference: The total situation. *International Journal of Psychoanalysis, 66*: 447–454.

Jozef, B. (1974). *O Espaço reconquistado* (2nd edition). Rio de Janeiro: Paz e Terra.

Jozef, B. (1980). *O Jogo mágico*. Rio de Janeiro: Livraria José Olímpio.

Jozef, B. (1986). *Romance Hispano–Americano*. São Paulo: Ática.

Jozef, B. (2005). *História da Literatura Hispano-Americana* (4th edition). Rio de Janeiro: Francisco Alves.

Kaës, R. (2009). *Les alliances inconscientes [Unconscious Alliances]*. Paris: Dunod.

Kestenberg, J. (1968). Outside and inside, male and female. *Journal of the American Psychoanalytic Association, 16*: 457–520.

King, P. (1978). Affective response of the analyst to the patient's communications. *International Journal of Psychoanalysis, 59*: 329–334.

Klein, M. (1929). Infantile anxiety-situations reflected in a work of art and in the creative impulse. In: *The Writings of Melanie Klein, Vol. 1* (pp. 210–218). London: Hogarth Press.

Klein, M. (1930). The importance of symbol formation in the development of the ego. In: *The Writings of Melanie Klein, Vol. 1* (pp. 219–232). London: Hogarth Press.

Klein, M. (1932). *The Psychoanalysis of Children. The Writings of Melanie Klein, Vol. 2*. London: Hogarth Press.

Klein, M. (1935). A contribution to the psychogenesis of manic-depressive states. *International Journal of Psychoanalysis, 16*: 145–174.

Klein, M. (1946). Notes on some schizoid mechanisms. In: J. Riviere (Ed.), *Developments in Psychoanalysis* (pp. 292–320). London: Hogarth Press.

Klein, M. (1948). A contribution to the theory of anxiety and guilt. *International Journal of Psychoanalysis, 29*: 114–123.

Klein, M. (1952). Some theoretical conclusions regarding the emotional life of the infant. In: *The Writings of Melanie Klein, Vol. 3* (pp. 61–93). London: Hogarth Press.

Klein, M. (1958). On the development of mental functioning 1. *International Journal of Psychoanalysis, 39*: 84–90.

Klein, M. (1961). *Narrative of a Child Analysis. The Writings of Melanie Klein, Vol. 4*. London: Hogarth Press.

Klein, M. (1975). *Envy and Gratitude and Other Works 1946–1963. The Writings of Melanie Klein, Vol. 3*. London: Hogarth Press.

Kline, N. S., & Clynes, M. (1961). Drugs, space and cybernetics: Evolution to cyborgs. In: B. E. Flaherty (Ed.), *Psychophysiological Aspects of Space Flight (Symposium Proceeedings)*. New York: Columbia University Press.

Kohon, G. (1984). Reflections on Dora: The case of hysteria. *International Journal of Psychoanalysis, 65*: 73–84. Also in: G. Kohon (Ed.), *The British School of Psychoanalysis: The Independent Tradition*. London: Free Association Books, 1986.

Kohon, G. (1999). *No Lost Certainties to Be Recovered*. London: Karnac.

Kohon, G. (2000). Dreams, symbolic impoverishment and the question of the other. In: R. J. Perelberg (Ed.), *Dreaming and Thinking* (pp. 73–90). London: Karnac.

Kohon, G. (2007). Borderline traces and the question of diagnoses. In: A. Green (Ed.), *Resonance of Suffering: Countertransference in Non-Neurotic Structures*. London: Karnac.

Kohon, G. (2016). *Reflections on the Aesthetic Experience: Psychoanalysis and the Uncanny*. London: Routledge.

Kohon, G. (2018). Bye-bye sexuality. In: R. J. Perelberg (Ed.), *Psychic Bisexuality: British–French Dialogue* (pp. 258–276). London: Routledge.

Kohon, S. (2014). Making contact with the primitive mind: The contact-barrier, beta-elements and the drives. *International Journal of Psychoanalysis, 95* (2): 245–270.

Kohut, H. (1977). *The Restoration of the Self*. New York: International Universities Press.

Kohut, H. (1984). *How Does Analysis Cure?* Chicago, IL: University of Chicago Press.

Kristeva, J. (1991). *Strangers to Ourselves*. New York: Columbia University Press.

Kristeva, J. (1995). *New Maladies of the Soul*. New York: Columbia University Press.

Kristeva, J. (1996). *Time and Sense: Proust and the Experience of Literature*. New York: Columbia University Press.

Kristeva, J. (2000). *The Sense and Non-Sense of Revolt*. New York: Columbia University Press.

Kristeva, J. (2012). *Hatred and Forgiveness*. New York: Columbia University Press.

Lacan, J. (1956–60). *The ethics of psychoanalysis. Seminars, Book VII*, trans, D. Porter. New York: Routledge, 1992.

Lacan, J. (1966 [1949]). Le stade du miroir comme formateur de la fonction du je. In: *Ecrits*. Paris: Éditions du Seuil.

Lacan, J. (1968). The phallic phase and the subjective import of the castration complex. In: J. Mitchell, & J. Rose (Eds.), *Jacques Lacan and the École Freudienne: Feminine Sexuality* (pp. 99–122). London: Penguin, 1982.

Lacan, J. (1973). *Le séminaire, Livre XI. Les quatre concepts fondamentaux de la psychanalyse*. Paris: Éditions du Seuil.

Lacan, J. (1977). *Ėcrits: A Selection*, trans. Alan Sheridan. London: Routledge.

Lacan, J. (1978). *Le séminaire, Livre II. Le moi dans la theorie de Freud et dans la technique de la psychanalyse*. Paris: Éditions du Seuil.

Lacan, J. (1981). *Le séminaire, Livre III. Les psychoses (1955–56)*. Paris: Éditions du Seuil.

Lacan, J. (1991). *The Seminar of Jaques Lacan, Book II. The Ego in Freud's Theory and in the Technique of Psychoanalysis, 1954–1955*, trans S. Tomaselli. New York: W. W. Norton.

Lacan, J. (1993). *The Seminar of Jaques Lacan, Book III. The Psychosis, 1955–56*, trans R. Grigg. London: Routledge.

Lacan, J. (1994). *Le Séminaire, Livre IV. La relation d'objet*. Paris: Éditions du Seuil.

Lacan, J. (1998). *The Seminar of Jacques Lacan, Book XX. On Feminine Sexuality: The Limits of Love and Knowledge, Encore*, trans. B. Fink. New York: W. W. Norton.

Lacan, J. (2004). *Le séminaire, Livre X: L'angoisse [The Seminar, Book X: Anxiety] [1962–63]*, ed. J. A. Miller. Paris: Seuil.

Lacan, J. (2005). *Des Noms-Du-Père*. Paris: Seuil.

La Fontaine, J. S. (1981). The domestication of the savage male. *Man, 16*: 333–349.

La Fontaine, J. S. (1985). Anthropological perspectives on the family and social change. *Quarterly Journal of Social Affairs, 1* (1): 29–56.

Laplanche, J. (1981). *The Unconscious and the Id*, trans. L. Thurston. London: Rebus, 1999.

Laplanche, J. (1987). *New Foundations for Psychoanalysis*, trans. D. Macey. Oxford: Blackwell, 1989.

Laplanche, J. (1999). *Essays on Otherness*. London: Routledge.

Laplanche, J. (2006). *L'Après-coup*. Paris: Presses Universitaires de France.

Laplanche, J. (2007). Gender, sex, and the sexual. *Studies in Gender and Sexuality, 8*: 201–219.

Laplanche, J., & Pontalis, J.-B. (1967). *The Language of Psychoanalysis*. London: Hogarth Press, 1973; reprinted London: Karnac, 1988.

Laufer, M. E. (1993). The female Oedipus complex and the relationship to the body. In: D. Birksted-Breen (Ed.), *The Gender Conundrum* (pp. 67–81). London: Routledge.

Leach, E. R. (1961). Two essays concerning the symbolic representation of time. In: *Rethinking Anthropology* (pp. 124–136). London: Athlone Press, 1971.

Leclaire, S. (1975). *On tue un enfant*. Paris: Éditions du Seuil.

Leclaire, S. (1980). Jerome, or death in the life of the obsessional. In: S. Schneiderman (Ed.), *Returning to Freud: Clinical Psychoanalysis in the School of Lacan* (pp. 94–113). New Haven, CT: Yale University Press.

Lemma, A. (2013). The body one has and the body one is: The transsexual's need to be seen. *International Journal of Psychoanalysis, 94* (2): 277–292.

Lemma, A. (2016). *The Black Mirror: Identity, Body, Technology*. Unpublished paper presented to UCL Conference, December.

Levine, H. B., Reed, G. B., & Scarfone, D. (Eds.) (2013). *Unrepresented States and the Construction of Meaning*. London: Karnac.

Lévi-Strauss, C. (1967). *The Elementary Structures of Kinship and Marriage*. Boston, MA: Beacon Press, 1969.

Lévi-Strauss, C. (1968). *Structural Anthropology, Vol. 1*. Harmondsworth: Penguin.

Limentani, A. (1979). The significance of the transsexual in relation to some basic psychoanalytic concepts. *International Review of Psycho-Analysis, 6*: 139–153.

Lorca, F. G. (1987). *Blood Wedding*. London: Methuen.

Magid, B. (1993). A young woman's homosexuality reconsidered. *Journal of the American Academy of Psychoanalysis and Dynamic Psychiatry, 21*: 421–432.

Masson, J. M. (Ed.) (1985). *The Complete Letters of Sigmund Freud to Wilhelm Fliess, 1887–1904*. Cambridge, MA: Belknap Press.

McDougall, J. (1986). Identifications, neoneeds and neosexualities. *International Journal of Psychoanalysis, 67*: 19–31.

McGuire, W. (Ed.) (1974). *The Freud/Jung Letters: The Correspondence between Sigmund Freud and C. G. Jung*. Princeton, NJ: Princeton University Press.

Mead, M. (1935). *Sex and Temperament in Three Primitive Societies*. London: Routledge & Kegan Paul.

Mitchell, J. (1984). The question of femininity and the theory of psychoanalysis. In: J. Mitchell (Ed.), *Women: The Longest Revolution. Essays in Feminism, Literature and Psychoanalysis* (pp. 295–313). London: Virago.

Mitchell, J. (1986). The question of femininity and the theory of psychoanalysis. In: G. Kohon (Ed.), *The British School of Psychoanalysis: The Independent Tradition* (pp. 381–398). London: Free Association Books.

Mitchell, J. (1999). Introduction. In *Psychoanalysis and Feminism* (pp. xv–xxxviii). Harmondsworth: Penguin.

Mitchell, J. (2000). *Mad Men and Medusas: Reclaiming Hysteria and the Effects of Sibling Relations on the Human Condition*. London: Penguin.

Mitchell, J. (2015). Debating sexual difference, politics and the unconscious: With discussant section by Jacqueline Rose. In: R. Duschinsky & S. Walker (Eds.), *Juliet Mitchell and the Lateral Axis* (pp. 77–99). New York: Palgrave.

Mitchell, J. (2018). Foreword. In: R. J. Perelberg (Ed.), *Psychic Bisexuality: A British–French Dialogue* (pp. xvi–xxiv). London: Routledge.

Money, J., & Ehrhardt, A. (1972). *Man and Woman, Boy and Girl*. New York: New American Library, 1974.

Money, J., Hampson, J. G., & Hampson, J. L. (1955). Hermaphroditism: Recommendations concerning assignment of sex, change of sex, and psychological management. *Bulletin of the Johns Hopkins Hospital, 97*: 284–300.

Morel, G. (2011). *Sexual Ambiguities*. London: Karnac.

Naidin, S. (2013). Desigualdade & diversidade. *Revista de Ciências Sociais da PUC-Rio, 12* (Jan/Dec): 191–204.

Naidin, S. (2016). *Tecnologias do corpo de do gênero. Um analise da construção de corporalidades femininas*. Doctoral thesis, Universidade do Estado do Rio de Janeiro.

Ogden, T. (1997a). Reverie and metaphor: Some thoughts on how I work as a psychoanalyst. *International Journal of Psychoanalysis, 78*: 719–732.

Ogden, T. (1997b). On holding and containing, being and reaming. *International Journal of Psychoanalysis, 85*: 1349–1364.

Oliver, K. (2012). Kristeva's maternal passions. *Journal of French and Francophone Philosophy*, 7 (1): 1–8.

Oppenheimer, A. (1991). The wish for a sex-change: A challenge to psychoanalysis? *International Journal of Psychoanalysis, 72*: 221–232.

Perelberg, R. J. (1990a). Equality, asymmetry, and diversity: On conceptualizations of gender. In: R. J. Perelberg & A. Miller (Eds.), *Gender and Power in Families* (pp. 34–60). London: Karnac, 2012.

Perelberg, R. J. (1990b). Introduction—I. In: R. J. Perelberg, & A. Miller (Eds.), *Gender and Power in Families* (pp. 1–7). London: Karnac, 2012.

Perelberg, R. J. (1995). A core phantasy in violence. *International Journal of Psychoanalysis, 76*: 1215–1231.

Perelberg, R. J. (1997a). Introduction to Part I. In: J. Raphael-Leff, & R. J. Perelberg (Eds.), *Female Experience: Three Generations of British Women Psychoanalysts on Work with Women* (pp. 21–35). London: Routledge.

Perelberg, R. J. (1997b). Introduction to Part III. In: J. Raphael-Leff, & R. J. Perelberg (Eds.), *Female Experience: Three Generations of Women Psychoanalysts on Work with Women* (pp. 218–227). London: Routledge.

Perelberg, R. J. (1997c). "To be—Or not to be—Here": A woman's denial of time and memory. In: J. Raphael-Leff, & R. J. Perelberg (Eds.), *Female Experience: Three Generations of Women Psychoanalysts on Work with Women* (pp. 60–76). London: Routledge.

Perelberg, R. J. (1999a). The interplay between identifications and identity in the analysis of a violent young man. *International Journal of Psychoanalysis, 80*: 31–45. Also in: *Time, Space and Phantasy* (pp. 66–86). London: Routledge, 2008.

Perelberg, R. J. (1999b). The interplay of identifications: Violence, hysteria and the repudiation of femininity. In: G. Kohon (Ed.), *The Dead Mother: The Work of André Green* (pp. 173–192). London: Routledge.

Perelberg, R. J. (2000). The oracle in dreams. In: R. J. Perelberg (Ed.), *Dreaming and Thinking* (pp. 109–128). London: Karnac.

Perelberg, R. J. (2003). Full and empty spaces in the analytic process. *International Journal of Psychoanalysis, 84*: 579–592.

Perelberg, R. J. (2004a). Narcissistic configurations: Violence and its absence in treatment. *International Journal of Psychoanalysis, 85*: 1065–1079.

Perelberg, R. J. (2004b). Psychoanalysis and feminism. In: A. Mijolla (Ed.), *International Dictionary of Psychoanalysis* (pp. 576–578). New York: McMillan Library Reference.

Perelberg, R. J. (Ed.) (2005). *Freud: A Modern Reader.* London: Wiley.

Perelberg, R. J. (2006). The controversial discussions and *après-coup*. *International Journal of Psychoanalysis, 87*: 1199–1220. Also in: *Time, Space and Phantasy* (pp. 106–130). London: Routledge, 2008.

Perelberg, R. J. (2007). Space and time in psychoanalytic listening. *International Journal of Psychoanalysis, 88*: 1473–1490. Also in: *Time, Space and Phantasy* (pp. 131–149). London: Routledge, 2008.

Perelberg, R. J. (2008a). *Time, Space and Phantasy*. London: Routledge.

Perelberg, R. J. (2008b). Introduction to Part I. In: J. Raphael-Leff & R. J. Perelberg (Eds.), *Female Experience: Four Generations of British Women Psychoanalysts on Work with Women* (pp. 21–35). London: Anna Freud Centre.

Perelberg, R. J. (2009a). Après-coup dynamique. Implications pour une theorie de la clinique. *Revue Française de Psychanalyse, 73*: 1583–1589.

Perelberg, R. J. (2009b). Murdered father, dead father: Revisiting the Oedipus complex. *International Journal of Psychoanalysis, 90*: 713–732.

Perelberg, R. J. (2011). "A father is being beaten": Constructions in the analysis of some male patients. *International Journal of Psychoanalysis, 92*: 97–116.

Perelberg, R. J. (2013). Paternal function and thirdness in psychoanalysis and legend: Has the future been foretold? *Psychoanalytic Quarterly, 82* (3): 557–585.

Perelberg, R. J. (2015). On excess, trauma and helplessness: Repetition and transformations. *International Journal of Psychoanalysis, 96*: 1453–1476.

Perelberg, R. J. (2016a). The enigma of Oedipus in social anthropology. In: *Murdered Father, Dead Father: Revisiting the Oedipus Complex* (pp. 95–124). London: Routledge.

Perelberg, R. J. (2016b). Glossary. In: *Murdered Father, Dead Father: Revisiting the Oedipus Complex* (pp. 189–196). London: Routledge.

Perelberg, R. J. (2016c). *Murdered Father, Dead Father: Revisiting the Oedipus Complex*. London: Routledge.

Perelberg, R. J. (2016d). Negative hallucinations, dreams and hallucinations: The framing structure and its representation in the analytic setting. *International Journal of Psychoanalysis, 97* (6): 1575–1590.

Perelberg, R. J. (2016e). The structuring function of the Oedipus complex. In: *Murdered Father, Dead Father: Revisiting the Oedipus Complex* (pp. 125–160). London: Routledge.

Perelberg, R. J. (2018a). Introduction: A psychoanalytic understanding of bisexuality. In: R. J. Perelberg (Ed.), *Psychic Bisexuality: A British–French Dialogue* (pp. 1–57). London: Routledge.

Perelberg, R. J. (Ed.) (2018b). *Psychic Bisexuality: A British–French Dialogue*. London: Routledge.

Perelberg, R. J., & Jozef, B. (2008). Time and memory in *One Hundred Years of Solitude*. In: R. J. Perelberg (Ed.), *Time, Space and Phantasy* (pp. 153–162). London: Routledge.

Pines, D. (1993). Early skin disorders and their effect on transference and countertransference. In: *A Woman's Unconscious Use of Her Body* (pp. 8–25). London: Virago.

Pirlot, G., & Cupa, D. (2012). *André Green. Les Grands concepts psychanalytiques*. Paris: Presses Universitaires de France.

Pontalis, J.-B. (1974). Bornes ou confins? In: *Aux limites de l'analysable* (pp. 5–16). Nouvelle Revue de Psychanalyse, 10. Paris: Gallimard.

Pontalis, J.-B. (1977). *Entre le rêve et la douleur*. Paris: Gallimard.

Preciado, P. B. (2008). *Testo Yonqui*. Barcelona: Espasa Libros.

Preciado, P. B. (2013). *Testo Junkie: Sex, Drugs, and Biopolitics in the Pharmacopornographic Era*. New York: The Feminist Press.

Quinodoz, D. (1998). A fe/male transsexual patient in psychoanalysis. *International Journal of Psychoanalysis, 79*: 95–111.

Racker, H. (1968). *Transference and Countertransference*. London: Hogarth Press; new edition, London: Karnac, 1982.

Raphael-Leff, J., & Perelberg, R. J. (Eds.) (1997). *Female Experience: Three Generations of British Women Analysts on Work with Women*. London: Routledge.

Raphael-Leff, J., & Perelberg, R. J. (Eds.) (2008). *Female Experience: Four Generations of British Women Psychoanalysts on Work with Women*. London: Anna Freud Centre.

Raymond, J. (1979). *The Transsexual Empire: The Making of the She-Male*. Boston, MA: Beacon Press.

Reed, G. S. (2002). The work of the negative. *Jounal of the American Psychoanalytic Association, 50*: 343–347.

Reed, G. S., & Baudry, F. D. (2005). Conflict, structure, and absence. *Psychoanalytic Quarterly, 74*: 121–155.

Richard, F. (2019) La bisexualité, l'inceste et la mort. Paper presented at the 79e Congres des Psychanalystes de Langue Francaise, Paris. Unpublished.

Riviere, J. (1936). A contribution to the analysis of the negative therapeutic reaction, 1. *International Journal of Psychoanalysis, 17*: 304–320.

Róheim, G. (1946). The Oedipus complex and infantile sexuality. *Psychoanalytic Quarterly, 15*: 503–508.

Róheim, G. (1950). *Psychoanalysis and Anthropology*. New York: International Universities Press, 1973.

Rolland, J.-C. (2006). *Avant d'être celui qui parle*. Paris: Editions Gallimard.

Rolland, J.-C. (2007). On the relevance of the borderline situation. In: A. Green (Ed.), *Resonance of Suffering* (pp. 195–202). London: International Psychoanalytical Association.

Rolland, J.-C. (2010). *Les yeux de l'âme*. Paris: Gallimard.

Rolland, J.-C. (2015). *Quatre essais sur la vie de l'âme*. Paris: Gallimard.

Rosaldo, M. Z., & Lamphere, L. (Eds.) (1974). *Women, Culture and Society*. Stanford, CA: Stanford University Press.

Rose, J. (1982). Introduction—II. In: J. Mitchell & J. Rose (Eds.), *Feminine Sexuality: Jacques Lacan and the École Freudienne* (pp. 27–57). London: Macmillan.

Rose, J. (2016). Who do you think you are? *London Review of Books, 38* (9): 3–13.

Rosenfeld, H. (1971). A clinical approach to the psychoanalytic theory of life and death instincts. *International Journal of Psychoanalysis, 52*: 169–178.

Rosenfeld, H. (1987). *Impasse and Interpretation*. London: Routledge.

Royle, N. (2003). *The Uncanny*. Manchester: Manchester University Press.

Sandler, J. (1976). Counter-transference and role-responsiveness. *International Review of Psycho-Analysis, 3*: 43–47.

Scarfone, D. (2013). From traces to signs: Presenting and representing. In: H. B. Levine, G. B. Reed, & D. Scarfone (Eds.), *Unrepresented States and the Construction of Meaning* (pp. 75–94). London: Karnac.

Schaeffer, J. (1986). Le rubis a horreur du rouge. Relation et contre-investissement hystérique. *Revue Française de Psychanalyse, 50*: 923–944.

Schaeffer, J. (1997). *Le refus du féminin*. Paris: Presses Universitaires de France.

Segal, H. (1957). Notes on symbol formation. *International Journal of Psychoanalysis, 38*: 391–397.

Segal, H. (1977). Countertransference. In: *The Work of Hanna Segal: A Kleinian Approach to Clinical Practice* (pp. 81–88). London: Karnac, 1986.

Shaviro, S. (1990). *Passion and Excess: Blanchot, Bataille, and Literary Theory*. Tallahassee, FL: Florida State University Press.

Shepherdson, C. (2001). Foreword. In: R. Harari, *Lacan's Seminar on Anxiety: An Introduction* (pp. ix–lxii). New York: Other Press.

Sluhovsky, M. (2017). The fascinating tale of Steve, a Shul-going Holocaust survivor, who became Stefanie, a Jew-hating lady. *Haaretz*, 28 June.

Sodré, I. (1994). Obsessional certainty versus obsessional doubt: From two to three. *Psychoanalytic Inquiry, 14*: 379–392.

Spillius, E. B. (1992). Clinical experiences of projective identification. In: R. Anderson (Ed.), *Clinical Lectures on Klein and Bion* (pp. 57–70). London: Routledge.

Spillius, E. B., Milton, J., Garvey, P., Couve, C., & Steiner, D. (2011). *The New Dictionary of Kleinian Thought*. London: Routledge.

Stein, R. (1995). Analysis of a case of transsexualism. *Psychoanalytic Dialogues, 5* (2): 257–289.

Stein, R. (1998). The poignant, the excessive and the enigmatic in sexuality. *International Journal of Psychoanalysis, 79*: 253–268.

Stein, R. (2008). The otherness of sexuality: Excess. *Jounal of the American Psychoanalytic Association, 56*: 43–71.

Steiner, J. (2005). Gaze, dominance and humiliation in the Schreber case. In: R. J. Perelberg (Ed.), *Freud: A Modern Reader* (pp. 189–205). London: Wiley.

Stoller, R. J. (1968). *Sex and Gender.* London: Karnac, 1984.

Stoller, R. J. (1975). *The Transsexual Experiment.* London: Hogarth Press.

Strachey, J. (1926). Editor's introduction. In: S. Freud, *Inhibitions, Symptoms and Anxiety. Standard Edition, 20*: 77–86.

Temperley, J. (2005). The analysis of a phobia in a five-year-old boy. In: R. J. Perelberg (Ed.), *Freud: A Modern Reader* (pp. 61–71). London: Wiley.

Thurman, J. (2008). First impressions: What does the world's oldest art say about us? *New Yorker*, 23 June.

Todd, J. M. (1986). The Veiled Woman in Freud's "Das Unheimliche". *Signs, 11*: 519–541.

Todorov, T. (1970). *The Fantastic: A Structural Approach to A Literary Genre*, trans. R. Howard. Ithaca, NY: Cornell University Press.

Torok, M. (1994). The illness of mourning and the phantasy of the exquisite corpse. In: N. Abraham & M. Torok (Eds.), *The Shell and the Kernel*, trans. N. Rand. Chicago, IL: University of Chicago Press.

Urribarri, F. (2005). Le cadre de la representation dans la psychanalyse contemporaine. In: F. Richard & F. Urribarri (Eds.), *Autour de l'oeuvre d'André Green* (pp. 201–216). Paris: Presses Universitaires de France.

Urribarri, F. (2013). *Dialoguer avec André Green.* Paris: Éditions d'Ithaque.

Vargas Llosa, M. (1971). *García Márquez. Historia de un Deicidio.* Barcelona: Barral editores.

Verhaeghe, P. (2001). *Beyond Gender. From Subject to Drive.* New York: Other Press.

Verhaeghe, P. (2009). *New Studies of Old Villains: A Radical Consideration of the Oedipus Complex.* New York: Other Press.

Williams, P. (2004). Incorporation of an invasive object. *International Journal of Psychoanalysis, 85*: 1333–1348.

Williams, P. (2005). Notes upon a case of obsessional neuroses. In: R. J. Perelberg (Ed.), *Freud: A Modern Reader* (pp. 177–188). London: Wiley.

Winnicott, D. W. (1960). Counter-transference. In: *The Maturational Processes and the Facilitating Environment: Studies in the Theory of Emotional Development* (pp. 158–165). London: Hogarth Press, 1965.

Winnicott, D. W. (1963). Communicating and not communicating leading to a study of certain opposites. In: *The Maturational Processes and the Facilitating Environment: Studies in the Theory of Emotional Development* (pp. 179–192). London: Hogarth Press, 1965.

Winnicott, D. W. (1971a). Creativity and its origins. In: *Playing and Reality* (pp. 65–85). London: Routledge.

Winnicott, D. W. (1971b). *Playing and Reality*. London: Tavistock Publications.

Zilkha, N. (2018). Stumbling blocks of the feminine, stumbling blocks of psychic bisexuality. In: R. J. Perelberg (Ed.), *Psychic Bisexuality: A British–French Dialogue* (pp. 151–169). London: Routledge.

Index

For Product Safety Concerns and Information please contact our EU representative GPSR@taylorandfrancis.com
Taylor & Francis Verlag GmbH, Kaufingerstraße 24, 80331 München, Germany

www.ingramcontent.com/pod-product-compliance
Lightning Source LLC
Chambersburg PA
CBHW060937160926
51501CB00060B/161
9780367253547